The Courage to Change

Dr. Sax Guthery Jr.

ISBN 978-1-0980-1681-4 (paperback)
ISBN 978-1-0980-1682-1 (digital)

Copyright © 2019 by Dr. Sax Guthery Jr.

All rights reserved. No part of this publication may be reproduced, distributed, or transmitted in any form or by any means, including photocopying, recording, or other electronic or mechanical methods without the prior written permission of the publisher. For permission requests, solicit the publisher via the address below.

Christian Faith Publishing, Inc.
832 Park Avenue
Meadville, PA 16335
www.christianfaithpublishing.com

Printed in the United States of America

Contents

Foreword 5
Abstract 7
Introduction 9
Chapter 1:   Deny Yourself 11
Chapter 2:   Break the Chain of Iniquity 19
Chapter 3:   Burn Notice 23
Chapter 4:   Breaking the Spirit of Whoredoms (Hosea 4:12) 31
Chapter 5:   Breaking the Soul Ties 42
Chapter 6:   Soul Ties, Fingerprints on Your Soul (Revelation).....51
Chapter 7:   Getting Your Soul Back 67
Chapter 8:   Breaking the Chain of the "I Can't Help Its" 75
Chapter 9:   Take Up Your Cross To Be a Prisoner of the Lord…(Matthew 16:24)..87
Chapter 10: The Cross of Loss 97
Chapter 11: The Cross of Shame, Fear, and Control 110
Chapter 12: Follow Me 122
Chapter 13: Put God First 132
Chapter 14: Entering into the Will of God 143
Chapter 15: Psalm 31:15, My Times are In His Hands… 153
Conclusion 157
Works Cited 161

FOREWORD

I want to thank my wife the late Pastor Helena M. Guthery, for her unwavering faith to God for me to be healthy and whole in God. Helena, your prayers did not go unanswered. I have, and I am becoming that Stallion that God showed you some years ago that I was to be. I thank you for every tear and every lesson you taught me regarding serving God. Your untimely death has been unfortunate for many, but your departure has, in some ways, caused us all to grow.

Helena, I thank you for the many conversation that we had before you left this earth—even those conversation that we had during the last days of your life while you were still in the hospital. You told me to not be surprised how people were to treat me after you were gone because your death was only going to bring out what was really in them all the time.

However, I thank God for all the test and trials I have had since your departure, and I now realize that all of my VICTORIES are in Jesus. "According to my earnest expectation and my hope, that in nothing I shall be ashamed, but that with all boldness, as always, so now also, Christ shall be magnified in my body, whether it be by life, or by death" Philippians 1:20, KJV.

I thank you for your love and your patience with me and the many wonderful years that we had the opportunity to experience the love of God together. Your wisdom has been paramount to many, and I thank God for seeing God's love and wisdom in full operation through you.

Abstract

Many times, we are faced with challenges in our lives that rock us to our very core. These challenges come for a variety of reasons if we are open and honest to face them. These challenges can leave us emotionally, physically, mentality, or spiritually bankrupt in our ability to handle these challenges by ourselves or within ourselves. I believe one of the greatest poverties that a man can experience is spiritual poverty. If it was physical poverty alone, a doctor or psychiatrist could help you. If it was emotional, a therapist or physiologist could walk you through a process of change. But whenever there is spiritual poverty, it will take God to bring you out of what you're in.

In this book, you will see that I faced many emotional, physical, and spiritual poverties. One thing to remember is that when this was all happening in my life, I did not have the answers that spoke to the problems. Understand that everything that happens to us naturally as believers, there is a spiritual response to it.

What you will see in the pages ahead is my inability to trust myself and my ability to put my total faith and trust in the Lord. When God normally shows you a picture of yourself, it can be very revealing and very ugly. Because in essence, when you take an honest look at yourself, what do you really see? Okay, you got to move past the skin and the makeup and the hair and look into the innermost part of your being. If you're willing and you're ready to move forward to the pages ahead, I will give you insights on how you can break certain chains in your life if you can be true and honest to yourself. And if you are honest, maybe, just maybe, you too will have The Courage to Change. Enjoy!

INTRODUCTION

I started writing this book after God had dealt with me regarding some issues in my life that I really, really needed to face. Since then, there have been several major things that have happened to shape the way of my approach in writing this book. However, going back to my original way of addressing this very serious introspection and outlook on myself and those around me, they have proven to be what I needed. I would like to say that I thank God for my grandson Joshua whom, at the time, I was babysitting. And while babysitting, I was on a extended fast seeking the mind of God regarding the direction for my life, and as Joshua was playing, he began to sing Tasha Cobb's song "Break Every Chain." Of course, I had heard the song before it had just come on the scene as a new song that was released, and the more he sang the song while jumping on and off of my bed, the song penetrated into my heart. And right then, I noticed what God was doing in my life. God was BREAKING EVERY CHAIN that held me captive, and the power of God fell on me like never before.

I thank Joshua Jr. for his obedience in sharing that song. In the pages that follows, you will begin to understand and watch as God unfold His Mercy and Grace and His Love in my life by bringing me out of places in my life that I did not even realize that I had, slipped into regarding the power of the enemy. One thing is for sure: when God begins to show you yourself most of the time, it's not a pretty sight, and you need the grace of God to bear it. So I would like for you to walk with me as I take you on a very vivid journey of my life and the bands of wickedness that was broken from off of my life and how God allowed me to walk in the freedom of His Word because He has and yet still does Break Every Chain in our lives so that we might be free to Worship Him in the Beauty of Holiness, but in order for God to do that, we will need The Courage to Change, which is the title of this book. I can only pray and hope that God inspires you to have The Courage to Change as well while you read the pages of this book.

Chapter 1

Deny Yourself

*If any man is to come after me let him deny himself
and take up his cross and follow me.*

—Matthew 16:24

Well, it all started one September while I was working for an adolescent childcare program for adjudicated youth in Detroit Michigan. We had just had a serious violation with one of the youths from our Abuse and Neglect Programs. It was a very serious case. However, I figured things would pan out because the licensing rules work a little different with that population. Two days after this incident, I was called into my boss's office. I thought that I was going to receive my evaluation that I had been waiting for, but to my surprise, I was told that I was being let go. I pleaded my case for a moment and even thought that the decision to let me go could or would be overturned. I stated to my boss, "Okay, give me a hug."

We embraced, and then it dawned on me that God was trying to tell me something. I had been here before. No, not with being fired from a position, but at this point in my life, it was something more going on with the things that were occurring in my life. I felt like I had given all of me to this job, my employees, to the administration, and mostly to the kids that were in that population. But yet,

I was still being fired, but for what? I had a list of accomplishments and programs and systems that I had put in place to make the overall environment for the children and the staff better, but once again, too me, this was not making sense. You see, I'm one of those people that when things happen, I question and analyze every area of the situation because sometimes, things that happen don't have to be your fault, and you have the right to respond to those incidents appropriately. But I really felt like if God would allow this to happen to me, He obviously is trying to get my attention for some unknown reason. But boy would I learn why this happen in the months to come.

So as I left the job, I was hurt and a little sad, but I felt this hope in me. You see, if you know anything about TROUBLE, you will realize when trouble comes in your life. It comes to get your undivided attention, and I mean I was as alert as I have ever been, and this trouble I now had had my undivided attention. How will I to pay my bills? My wife was sick and in the hospital every other day. How was I to take care of her? How was I going to pay my three-car notes and insurance?

These are questions that people may ask every day, but for me, my material needs were real, and at the time, I didn't know what I was going to do. Something similar like this had happen some years back. However, I did not fully understand then what was to be understood in the months to come. Sometimes, there are lessons to be learned, but we, as believers, don't stop long enough to learn the lesson or ask the right questions. I'm sure if you stop and think long and hard, you will see patterns of God trying and attempting to get your attention through a job, a friend, or a relationship that you're in and you know it's no good for you. But year after year, you refuse to believe the signs, and you continue to stay in the same way of life stuck in a rut. There is a Scripture in Jeremiah 8:20 that says, "The harvest has past, the summer has ended, and yet we are still not saved." Year after year, we may have told God that we were going to get our lives together and do better, but the harvest has passed, the summer has ended, and nothing has changed.

I was pretty distraught about the entire situation, so I said to myself that I was going to go on a fast and pray and seek the Lord not only about a job but about the plans that He had for my life. Proverbs 19:21 says, "Many are the plans in a man's heart but the counsel of the Lord shall stand." In Greek, the word counsel means PURPOSE, and it's true that God has a purpose and plan for all of our lives that will supersede our plans and purpose for our lives if we let Him lead us. The key here is, we have to be open and ready and able to hear Him when He calls. So after going through the stages of calling unemployment and all of that stuff, I was sleeping one night, and I heard a voice saying to me if any man is to come after me, deny himself, take up his cross, and follow me. When I finally got up the next morning, I ran to get my Bible, and sure enough, there it was in Matthew 16:24 that says, "If any man is to come after me let him deny himself and take up his cross and follow me."

I began to do research on what it meant to come after the Lord, but the thing that stuck out to me the most was the word DENY. I mean, over the next couple of weeks and even today, the word DENY was like STOP and a neon sign in my life. You see, we have this grown complex in our society today that we feel because we are grown, we can say and do whatever it is that we want to. This would include how we talk and deal with people in general. So the word DENY for me was like a cross would be for a sinner. It meant that I can't receive nor have the pleasures that I want to have. I guess the real question is, who tells you, a grown person, what to do? Or should I say when you're grown, I mean real grown, who tells you to do anything that you would listen to?

So I decided to run research on what the word deny means, and the best definition that stuck out to me the most was this: the word "deny means to stop doing what you want to do." Woo wee. You mean that I have to stop doing what I want to do? Yes, that's what God was saying to me. Stop doing things your way. Stop living life by your own terms. And stop not listening to the many signs and words that was shared with me through the years to live my life the way He wanted me to. Deny, Deny, Deny. Isn't it amazing that we want to control everything and everybody that has something to do with us in our lives, but we will not stop long enough to let God control us or organize things that He wants and know that we need for our lives?

Here I am with a master's degree, seminary trained, degrees, and certifications. I have enough plagues of accolades to fill and entire wall, but I can't even stop doing what I want to do for the Lord.

See, you must understand that I had been saved for years, filled with God's Spirit, spoke in tongues as the Spirit gives utterance, but I'm now faced with a dilemma. I have no job. My grandmother died earlier this year, my step-son just died two months before I was fired, my mother fell in her apartment because she had a stroke and was now in a comma, and now this. I was used to making a certain amount of money to pay for a lifestyle that I appreciated having. My wife was sick, and her heart is only working at 10 percent, and she can die at any time. Yes, God had healed her in the past since she was diagnosed and was given a date to die in 2005, and she is a walking miracle and a testimony of God's unfailing love. But now God is asking me to DENY myself, stop doing what I want to do, and follow Him. I can imagine the impact of the crowd that was following Jesus when He spoke these words. How can we follow Jesus with all of the baggage we have? Okay, how could I follow Jesus with all the baggage I had "saved but not delivered" dealing with weakness in my flesh and the iniquities of my father's.

In my mind, it was going to be hard to deny myself. Who don't want to put themselves in the best position to succeed no matter what arena were talking about? So I said to my wife and Pastor Helena Guthery, "I can't do that. I can't deny myself."

And she said "don't say that" as though God was going to teach me a lesson that I did not want to know.

I said to her, "I can't deny myself, but with the help of God, I can."

Why would Jesus want me to deny myself when he has made us to be more than conquerors through Him? Why deny ourselves and not fulfill ourselves with whatever it is in front of us? Why take up a cross of death instead of living life to the fullest? Why be a follower when we are destined to lead?

It's a fair question to ask, and the answer is related to our navigation problem. You see, we think that we are somewhere that we're not. The answer is because of the prevailing current problems in our society of human attitudes which were what Jesus calls "adulterous and sinful generation."

Our society is an adulterous generation, and a recent survey shows that about half the adults in this country believe adultery to be okay in some circumstance. The good news about marriage reveals the divorce rate among those active in their church is 227 to 50 percent lower than among nonchurchgoers. But by adultery here, I believe Jesus means more. He is referring as the prophets often did to people who had been unfaithful to God and gone with false gods of money, sex, and power.

Same sex marriage had been approved (Bible.Org). The LGBTQ+ community now has rights. None of this was as prevalent in 2013. I'm not judging anybody. That's already been done in the Word. But this is why Jesus had to be radical in His approach, and it's still relevant today. The idea for anyone in today's society to Deny themselves goes against the current thinking. In our society today, identity is so important that people are stealing another person's identity. One of the weapons that the enemy is fighting with us today is the ability to attempt to wipe away your personality and your sense of self-worth.

The enemy does this in how we view ourselves. When we don't deny ourselves, we become part of the problem just like in Numbers 13:28,31. Moses and the children of Israel traveled from Mount Sinai in hopes of possessing the land of promised to them, according to the divine covenants made with Abraham, Isaac, and Jacob (see Exodus 3:16–17; Exodus 33:1–3). Before entering the land, Moses sent out twelve men as spies to explore the land, and after being gone for forty days, they came back with grapes and pomegranates to show the people that the land did flow with milk and honey.

However, ten of them also stated that the walls were great and the people were too great of a people for them to conquer. Joshua and Caleb were the only two that believed that they could, with the help of God, overthrow these people. But because of their fear and not faith, their report was that they saw themselves as grasshoppers in the sight of their enemy and that there was no way that they could win over them, and they would rather die in the desert than try to defeat these people. Here's the point that I want to make. As long as you see yourself less than your problem, you're always going to have them problems. How you view yourself is so important for your future and your Victories in God. It is important that you see yourself greater than the problem in order to defeat the problem, but you can't do that if you're not willing to deny yourself. Even if you can't see yourself greater than the problem, at least know that your "God" is greater than any problem in your life.

Yet Jesus is saying that we have to deny ourselves. Do you understand just how hard that really is? Well, if you never thought about it, think of it like this. To deny yourself means when you think to do something right or wrong, stop for a moment and ask yourself if what you're about to do is going to bring God Glory or Shame. Does that really stop you from doing what your flesh wants to do? Even for the people who do stop and ask themselves this question, denying oneself is a drastic answer to a drastic problem. But consider taking up your cross. Does that mean death?

Just less than a year ago this year, there were several terrorist attacks. And since the most recent one's in the United States, there have been several more. We revere our Christian martyrs, but in today's society, the language of those who claim to be martyrs are the suicide bombers. Is this surely what Jesus was saying? And yet Jesus himself, who lived life to the fullest of his purpose and who was surely one the most life-affirming people in history, died with what appeared to be an untimely death (Bible.Org). By taking up our cross, we declare ourselves to be willing to share in Christ's humiliation and suffering and death just as we share in his life. As I said before, I can't deny myself. I'm exhausted just thinking about all of these things. It's too hard to do. I can't deny myself and take up a cross and follow Jesus. I can't do it without his help, but with his help, "I can do all things through Christ that strengthens me" (Philippians 4:19). Yet the word "deny" is burning in my head and spirit like a neon sign.

The definition of Deny is one that refuses to admit the truth or existence of something. You can't come to God or truly understand your purpose in life if you don't have faith to believe that in God is your future. Hebrews 11:6 says that without faith, it is impossible to please God because anyone who comes to God must believe that He "exists" and that he is a rewarder of them that diligently "earnestly" seek him. Deny means to contradict, challenge, counter, oppose, rebut, or be in contest about. Think of it. Until we come into the light of God's glorious truth, we spend most of our time contradicting, challenging, and even opposing the plan of God in our lives.

Years ago, I brought a Rottweiler dog. I mean, I paid $1500 for that dog. He was from a champion bloodline, and I had information on who his parents were and their pedigree, so I took him to a trainer. And this trainer not only helped train your dog, but they train you to train your dog. So I would go to the training, and there were other dogs there, and we would be training our dogs on socialization and obedience, and my dog knew nine commands in "German," and he knew how to sit, stay, lay, heel, come, go, surround, escort, protect, and attack.

If our dog did good in class, we would get first, second, third, and fourth place ribbons for their learning and success. One day, God dealt with me about me. He said to me, "You want your dog to obey you because you provide for him. You have paid for him. You have paid for all this training. He knows right from wrong. He only obeys your voice and your commands. He even know hand signals and obeys them."

God said, "Just like the dog, I want to know when you are going to obey me. When are you going to let me control your life and take you where I want you to go? And when I say sit, you sit. And when I say go, you go."

God went on to say to me, "I paid for you with my son's death on Calvary. You were bought with a price. You belong to me just like all of creation."

But from all of our actions of doing what we want to do, God cannot get us to DENY ourselves so that he can live through us to accomplish His will on earth. Then God really got me and said, "You have even taken your tithe money sometimes to pay for forty or sixty pound bags of dog food. You have even robbed me of my tithe to make sure that the dog eats."

But what my dog did not know is that sometimes, he was eating by grace because dog food can be very expensive. God said, "What you don't realize is that you are living by grace because my protection from demonic forces and my own son's blood was and is very, very, expensive."

1st Corinthians 6:20 says, "You were brought with a price. Therefore, honor God with your bodies." You have a debt that you could not pay, and God covered the tab for you. So you see, people, we owe God.

Deny means to stop doing what you want to do because the conflict that you are having is between you and God. You must surrender your will and give your heart to God, and He will make the necessary arrangements of change in your life.

Remember the Scripture says, "If anyone is to come after me, let him deny himself and take up his cross and follow me" (Matthew 16:24). This may be the most important description of what it means to be a follower of Jesus in the entire Gospel. Yet most of us have no idea of what it truly means. We understand the imagery, but we don't know how to live it out.

Deny or restrain means to refuse to give or grant yourself something. Deny means self-denial. Have you ever met anyone who doesn't want to experience self-fulfillment? The only path to self-fulfillment is self-denial. There is no other way to get there. While self-denial may sound miserable, it's actually wonderful. We simply must deny ourselves of those things which are temporarily pleasurable but eternally painful. We deny the desires of our flesh. We deny the temptation of sin. We desire to be like Him. We make up our mind to serve Him only. We refuse to settle for anything other than our NEW and nothing less than the best that God has to offer us of His good blessing and perfect will.

Chapter 2

Break the Chain of Iniquity

*Training us to renounce ungodliness and
worldly passions, and live self-controlled, upright,
and godly lives in the present age.*

—Titus 2:12

The term <u>mystery</u> has reference to some operation or plan of God hitherto unrevealed. The mystery of iniquity (the father's sins visited on the children) is the method God uses to enforce His moral laws—Ten Commandments. "For I thy God is a jealous God, visiting the iniquity of the fathers upon the children unto the third and fourth generation of them that hate me" (Exodus 20:5).

You can see the iniquities of our Father's play out in our lives so clearly but don't understand or miss the opportunity to break those (generationally curses). A lot of us are going through things in our lives that can't or seem like they can't be broken. For instance, your father or grandfather was an alcoholic, and you wonder why you drink. You keep telling yourself that you are a social drinker, but when things are not going right in your life, you turn to drinking to anesthetize your pain. What you don't realize is that in some cases, this is the sin of your father in operation, and what your father did when he did not know how to cope with his pain, or that's what your grandfather did when he could not deal with issues in life. And now here you are—two generations from your grandfather—and you are doing the same thing and falling into the same lifestyle that ultimately could have taken their lives. It wasn't the bottle that killed him. It was the iniquity that drove him further and further away from God. "For the wages of sin is death but the gift of God is eternal life in Christ Jesus" (Romans 6:23).

That's what I meant early on when I was talking about being in a certain situation before. It's a place and time in which you know that something is happening in your life that is out of your control, and it's an opportunity for you to handle things the way you always did. Or it's a change for you to totally depend on God for your solution to your problems.

You see, iniquity is weakness that we have in a particular area of our nature that is born in us as a result of the sins of our forefathers. Psalms 51:5 says, "Behold, I was shaped in iniquity; and in sin did my mother conceive me." Iniquity is born in us through our parents. If we fail to recognize and confess our iniquities to Jesus, we become prone to the weaknesses found in our ancestors. And in turn, our children and grandchildren will manifest these same weaknesses.

Iniquity differs from sin because it is the breeding ground for sin, and it is in this area that Satan tempts us to transgress against God's laws. Sin is the willful and actual transgression of God's laws. Iniquity is the weakness in us in a particular area of life because of the sin of our forefathers. Original sin is the total corruption of our nature because of the enmity (hostility against God) that is in us as a result of the sin of Adam (Gruits, pg.141).

It's important to understand iniquities because they are weakness in your flesh that keeps popping up, so you can take them to God for deliverance. For instance, you wonder why you feel as though you always need to have a man, boyfriend, or someone in your life. It really could stem from rejection or abandonment issues that you may have had in your adolescent years or with your parents. But in order to really examine it, take a deeper look at it. You must ask yourself the question of what you fear the most. For some, they will say loneness or being alone or not feeling valued and wanted to get back from someone. What they have put out to everyone is love that came from their hearts only to be dissatisfied and unloved and unappreciated. And ultimately, you feel abused, used, and, in some cases, destitute because you don't understand why others can have healthy relationship but you don't. If you're honest with yourself, it could be that God has been trying to tell you something for years, and you fail to recognize that it was him. God got you out of the bad situation not for you to go back into another. God got you out so that you could DENY yourself. Pick up your cross and follow Him.

See? The mistake that most of us make is we think that when something goes wrong in our lives and we hear from God and feel like we need to do something, normally the first thing we do is find a church to go to. And before long, we feel good. But then our desires begin to focus on what our needs are, and, in some cases, it's to be with someone. Then church become a breeding ground for us to get a hook up with someone in the church, and we say to ourselves that God must be in it because He led me to come to church, so my husband must be here. But what we don't realize is that God did not lead us to a church to find a man or a woman. He led us to the church to find Him. We are the ones that fell back into the same old patterns, iniquities, and weakness in our flesh that keep popping up, so we can bring them to Him. So when that relationship doesn't work, we're back to square zero because we have not yet learned how to DENY ourselves.

Isaiah 6:5 then said, "I, Woe is me! For I am undone; because I am a man of unclean lips, and I dwell in the midst of a people of unclean lips: for mine eyes have seen the king, The Lord of Hosts."

> For that which I do allow not: for what I would, that I do not; but what I hate, that I do. If then I do that which I would not, I consent unto the law that is good. Now then it is no more I that do it, but sin that dwelleth in me. (Romans 7:15–17)

God is after the sin that is dwelling in you. That sin that is a part of your daily walk for some and for others. It only comes out when there is and urge for something—be it sex, money, prestige, power, or to be a victim. We must be careful to listen to see if God is trying and have been trying to tell us something. Ultimately, God wants us saved, healed, and delivered, but in some cases, we don't have a clue what we really need to be healed from, so God sends unusual tests in trials in our lives to get us to take an honest look at who we are and, more importantly, as to who He Is.

Chapter 3

Burn Notice

I can do all things through Christ that strengths me.

—Philippians 4:13

There is a TV show called *Burn Notice*. It's about a spy who was given notice that everyone that he ever dealt with now knows that he is/was a spy. He was left with nothing. Not even his own identity because everything that he ever did is/was a lie.

As Christians, we have been indoctrinated to believe that if our life does not portray that of blessing and untold wealth, it's obvious that God must not be with us. In today's society, if your life does not portray signs of blessing and material wealth, then truly, God might not be with you. The Christian church has also portrayed that if your life is not on the mountain top, then there must be something wrong with you or your living, or you must be practicing some kind of sin that's stopping your blessings. A portion of that is true in a sense that God loves the person but hates the sin.

However, one thing the church does not teach is what happens when you fail in certain areas of your life. When it feels and looks as if you're losing everything, and you're not having a mountain top experience, and you're not sure when you are going to come of out this cycle because yes, a portion of your life is challenged with iniquities and weakness in your flesh and emotions. You feel as though you are losing on all sides. You may be jobless. You may be in a bad relationship that feels like bondage to you. You may not stop drinking, and you know it's killing you. You may even feel as though you want a husband or wife, but you keep attracting and hooking up with men or women that never mean you any good. What happens when you're losing, but all you ever been taught is to win. Maybe—just maybe—God has given you a Burn Notice. God has exposed you in a way that will ultimately bring Him Glory. You don't see it right now, but your test will be a testimony if you chose God.

A Burn Notice is exposure to your problems. When I say exposure, I'm talking about the things that you use to do that was against Him and got away with it. At least you thought you were getting away with them. You find that you can't get away with it anymore because God has placed an expiration date on that offense. Let me explain. People don't stop sinning because they got caught cheating on their wife or got caught stealing money from their job, or the pastor saw them drinking while they were out at the mall. People stop sinning when the spirit of the Lord allows them to be exposed, and God speaks a Word to your spirit that says DENY yourself. Stop doing what you're doing. You being caught doing whatever you were doing is a chance for you to rid yourself from the bad choices that you made.

Exposure of your sin is supposed to get you to have some disclosure of yourself. Self-examination of your inner self will allow you to look at the real reason to why you have committed the offense in the first place. I have a question for you. Who stirred up the Hell or Trouble in Job's life? We are so quick to say, without a doubt, that Job was blessed by God because Job records his substance in Job 1:3 which says, "and he owned seven thousand sheep, three thousand camels, and five hundred yoke of oxen, and five hundred donkeys, and had a large number servants, and a great household; so much that this man was the greatest of all the men in the East."

So it's not like Job was not blessed with substance, and I'm sure people in the church community spoke well of him, but oh, how people's views of you change when your substance change. We will come back to this point later. However, look at Verse 8: "and the

Lord said unto Satan, hast thou considered my servant Job, that there is none like him in the earth, a perfect and an upright man, one that feareth God, and escheweth evil?"

Let's examine. The Scripture that God said to Satan "have you considered my servant Job?" explains that it was God and not Satan to allow Job to go through a season of testing, so the exposure to trouble, pain, sickness, and disease could bring forth the disclosure and, ultimately, the closure of who Job was and who God is to Job. Satan will never turn down the opportunity to bring shame, harm, or fear to us. But what's remarkable about the Book of Job is that God never intended on Job being lost to Him. Another question that I have is, what happens when God have faith in you? Could it be that no matter what circumstances you find yourself in, God has enough faith in you to know that eventually, you will find your way back to Him? Maybe it's because it's like the Scripture Philippians 2:13 that says, "For it is God who works in you to will and to act in order to fulfill his good purpose" (King James Version, Life Application Bible).

When God spoke with me about denying myself, it was the exposure of my problems and circumstance that allowed me to take an honest look at who I was and what I was doing. But in the middle of all that I was going through, God never meant for me to be totally lost. And, my friend, so it is with you. You may have been through some very hard times and you may be having some hard times as you read this book, but what' I'm telling you is that at the end of your test, if you choose God, you will come to realize that He always chose you to be victorious, and you have been given a Burn Notice so that your eyes can be open to the fact that it was God that has been keeping you all the time.

Let's go deeper. 1 Corinthians 3:10–16 where Verse 13 says, "Every man's work shall be manifested: for the day shall declare it, because it shall be revealed by fire; and the fire shall try every man's work of what sort it is."

Now for the politically correct, this Scripture is just a pretext to a context, but I want to deal with this section of the Scripture first. Notice that regardless of what you do, meaning treating people right, loving people right, your vocation at work, your giving of yourself at church even your sins, and your family, if you have not built your foundation on Jesus Christ, every man's work shall be manifested for the day shall declare it, and it will be revealed or tired by fire. What fire? The concepts are the Baptism of the Holy Spirit and Fire. However, there are few that understand what this means.

In essence, it means that God will allow unusual test and trials in your life to burn out of you things that are not of Him. Here's the thing. Verse 10 says, according "to the grace of God which is given unto me, as a wise master builder, I have laid the foundation, and another buildeth thereon. But let every man take heed how he buideth thereupon."

"For other foundation can no man lay than that is laid, which is Jesus Christ" (verse 11),

"now if any man builds upon this foundation gold, silver, precious stones, wood, hay stubble" (v 12).

"Every man's works shall be made manifested" (v 13).

The context is that if you don't build your foundations on Jesus, it will be tested by fire, and other foundations will not be able to withstand the test because God himself is not a part of that foundation.

You cannot build a foundation with another family when you have a family of your own that you have not supported or protected, and you cannot think that the test of times is not going to try that foundation. You cannot be in a relationship with two women and think that your heart will not be tried with fire. What fire am I talking about? I'm talking about the TRUTH. No matter what situation you find yourself in, you must always deal with the truth.

If you're a dog, deal with the fact that you are a dog and have hurt or misused people, and the Bible says "that the truth will set you free" (John 8:32). This is not to say that you are beyond help, but the phrase always deal with the truth if your honest will bring introspection to how you look and perceive yourself to be with an honest set of eyes. Normally, when we judge ourselves, we do so with emotions, feelings of who hurt us, or what has transpired in our lives to the reason to why we did some of the things we have done. But God's Word says that when you judge including yourself, use Righteous

Judgment. "Stop judging by the mere appearances, but instead judge correctly, or the New Living Translation says, look beneath the surface so you can judge correctly" (John 7:24). A lot of times, people say I'm this way or that way because someone hurt me, or I didn't have a father to tell me how to treat women, or I saw my father doing this or acting this way, so that's why I do it. Each one of us has to answer to God for the deeds that we do in these bodies. When we stand before God, we can't say to Him, "God, I beat my girlfriend because I saw my father beating my mother."

In some case as described early, that could be a generational curse in operation, but the Bible also teaches us in Ezekiel 18:1,4:

> The word of the Lord came to me: "what do you people mean by quoting this proverb about the land of Israel: The parents eat sour grapes and the children's teeth are set on edge"? As I live declare the Lord, you will no longer quote this proverb in Israel. For everyone belongs to me, the parent as well as the child—both alike belong to me. The soul that sinneth shall surely die.

In other words, this was a curse that the sins of our parents are visited upon us. In some, regarding that is still true in terms of iniquities. We have kids today that are seeing things in the Spirit Realm. One of the most important things we can do is tell our children we believe them when they say they are seeing something scary even when our adult eyes don't see it (Greenwood, pg.14).

We have failed to see through the sins of our past to identify with our children now. However, your father's sins are not predicated upon his father's sins no more than your sins are predicated upon your Fathers sin. Every man and woman, boy or girl, have to answer to God for the deeds that they have done. So it is true with you and me. Some of you may have never knew your dad should you be held liable for what he did or didn't do when it comes to his sin.

No, but every action does have a consequence because sin has wages, and you will get paid for every deed you do in these bodies, good or bad. Romans 6:23 tells us that the wages of sin is death but the gift of God is eternal life through Jesus Christ our Lord. "Do not deceive yourself God is not mocked what a man soweth that shall he also reap" (Galatians 6:7). Our earlier Scripture regarding building on the right foundation goes on to say, "Know ye not that ye are the temple of God, and the spirit of God dwells in you? If any man defile the temple of God, him shall God destroy; for the temple of God is holy, which temple are you" (I Corinthians 3:18).

If you truly belong to God, it's only a matter of time before all of your works are tested to see what sort of work it is. In some cases, your works will be burned, but you yourself can be saved. In other words, you could have had good intentions in everything that you have done and you may have got caught up in life's struggles when it came to your feelings, emotions, or just life itself that caused you to make the choices that you did. But every choice you ever made will be tried by fire to see if it was the right choice. What God was saying to me when he told me to DENY myself was that I was and had made a lot of wrong choices, and now was the time in my life where He had put an expiration date on my usual choice, and He wanted me to choose Him because my choices, even though I was saved but not delivered, could cause me to be lost. "Ever learning but never coming into the knowledge of the truth" (2 Timothy 3:7).

1st Corinthians 3:18–23 ends with these words:

> Let no man deceive himself, if any among you seem to be wise in this world, let him become a fool, that he may be wise. For the wisdom of this world is foolishness with God. For it is written, He take the wise in their own craftiness. And again, The Lord know the thoughts of the wise, that they are vain. Therefore let no man glory in men. For all things are yours whether Paul, or Apollos, or Cephas, or the world, or life, or death, or things present, or things to come; all are yours; and ye are Christ's, and Christ is God's.

What Paul is saying here is that both life and death are ours while nonbelievers are victims of life swept along by its current with problems and circumstances and wondering if there is meaning to it. Believers can use life well because we understand that its true purpose is to align us with God and to bring us in oneness with Him. Nonbelievers can only fear death. For believers, however, death holds no fear because Christ has conquered all fear. 1st John 4:18 says, "For there is no fear in love for perfect love cast out all fear. He that fears it not made perfect in love."

For believers, death is only the beginning of eternal life with God. So Paul urged the Corinthians to think of him, Peter, and Apollos as mere servants of Christ entrusted with God's mysteries. A servant does what his master tells him to do. We must do what God tells us to do in the Bible and through the Holy Spirit. Every day God presents us with needs and opportunities that challenge us to do what we know is right. And even in these, we sometimes make wrong decisions and choices that, for some, tie our lives up for years.

Well, God wants to break every chain in your life, but He does that by getting your undivided attention. Usually, that comes with and through trouble, and then comes a Word from God through nature, through a person, or from God Himself telling you what He has told me. Deny yourself and stop doing what you want to do because I have work for you to do for the Kingdom of God. But many of us never accomplish our purpose because we never let go of this world and what we want to do.

Think about it. How many times have you seen or heard this from someone or on a post on Facebook saying, "so and so is 'doing me.' Oh, come on. I know you said it before that you were doing you." But sometimes, when we speak, it is indicative of our character. We solidify the curse of rebellion that is working in us because that's exactly what we are doing—doing us, and that's what God hates.

Man was never created to do HIM. Man was created to do God's Will. And it's unfortunate that every time we try to do us, it ends up in total failure—my life included. And then we are left with a choice to continue to do us, and it may, most likely, get worst before we surrender our will to the will of God and let Him lead us.

What I have found is, a very few people have ever really given God total control of their lives because we live in a society where there is a me factor but not a we factor. We never stop and wonder if we could be further along with our lives if we would just surrender to the will of God.

I used to be one of those people self-centered and self-absorbed. It was always about me—what I needed, what I wanted, and what I had to have in order to promote me—until God spoke to my heart and said, "if any man is to come after me let him DENY himself. Take up your cross, and follow me. For what does it profit a man to gain the entire world and lose his soul or what shall you give in exchange for his soul" (Matthew 16:24).

I have never been the same since God has spoken this word to me because it was then with all of the trails, tribulations, and circumstances that I had going on in my life that I stopped playing church, and I heard the chains breaking off of me in the spirit realm, and I came alive to what God was doing in my life. He was saving me from me, but He was also saving me from Him and his wrath if I did not surrender to His Will. "Humble yourself, under the mighty power of God, and at the right time He will lift you" (1 Peter 5:6).

In order to humble yourself and if you are willing, you must first accept the Burn Notice. That means that you have been exposed. Exposure always comes with a choice. You can choose to continue to walk in sin, or you can use this exposure to DENY yourself and get out of the mess.

Chapter 4

Breaking the Spirit of Whoredoms (Hosea 4:12)

*For if you live accordingly to the flesh you shall die,
but if by the Spirit you put to death the deeds
of the body, you will live.*

—Romans 8:13

The Spirit of Whoredom does not only affect those who engage in prostitution or prevision. The Spirit of Whoredoms can be Spiritual as well as Physical Bondage. The Book of Hosea points to such a case.

"My people ask counsel at their stocks, and their staff declareth unto them: {witchcraft} for the spirit of whoredoms hath caused them to err, and they have gone a whoring from under their God" (Hosea 4:12, King James Version) (Robeson, pg.72).

"They will not frame their doings to turn unto their God; for the spirit of whoredoms in the midst of them, and they have not known the Lord" (Hosea 5:4).

Hosea's marriage to a harlot illustrated to the nation what they were doing when they forsook God to embrace the idols and false gods of their neighboring nations. It's important for me to paint a picture of what the job and role of the prophet was in these biblical times so that we can understand the call or task that was at hand for Hosea moving forward (Connor, pg.148).

The earlier prophets and the prophets of the Bible lives were usually an expression of what God desired for His people and about their relationship with Him and about the economic, political, physical, and spiritual situation of Israel. Real prophets shift nations. They came against governments declaring, thus, said the Lord.

Prophets were not beyond their challenges. Most of the scholars, priests, and kings resented them because they did things that they could not control. The prophets' entire lives were incorporated in their prophetic expression. With some prophets like Isaiah, his children were named to depict Israel's future. In many cases with prophets, their kids and their wives were included.

The prophets were responsible for what we call Bible Religion. They were the ones that adhered to Monotheists, the worship of one God. They were the spiritual conscience of Israel. They were the ones that reminded Israel that God will be your God, but you must exclusively be His people. The prophets, in most cases, were also responsible for the written text. As they said it, they wrote it, and if they didn't write it, they had students writing for them.

Hosea felt the shame and agony on a physical level with his harlot wife (Gomer) that God experiences when His people are unfaithful to Him in their pursuit of other gods. Although we may not actually offer sacrifices to a physical idol, whatever comes between us and our relationship to God is still an idol and, thus, a form of spiritual adultery although sex may not be involved. Whatever rules us is our god—be it food, sex, perversions, past hurts, abuse, sports, money power, or the pursuit of a career, video games, and electronic devices such as cell phones, tablets, television, a possession, our children, a religion, or a cause (Greenwood, pg. 44).

What Dominates You?

Have you ever taken time out to stop to see what really dominates you? What are you really full of? Or better yet, who are you really full of? Not who the Bible says that you are, but who are you really? You can tell who a person is by understanding what a person does with most of his/her time.

A real mother spends all of her time mothering. That does not mean that she cannot work, own a business, or pursue her dreams. But what it does mean is that at the end of the day, she is still a mother. She still knows how to speak to the needs of all of the kids that she has mothered. And working or anything else, for that matter, does not stop her from knowing how to care for her family. Whatever dominates you or whatever you spend most of your time doing, that's what you are or will become.

Apostle Paul makes this observation regarding what dominates you when he said in 1 Corinthians 6:12 that "all things are lawful unto me, but all things are not expedient: all things are lawful for me, but I will not be brought under the power of any." In other words, what Apostle Paul was saying is, it's important to do all the things that we may feel is needed for home, work, and business. However; none of these things have to consume us where we are out of touch with our families and, more importantly, out of touch with our God.

Television, sports, food, video games, shopping, sex, etc. are not evil in themselves. They only become a problem to us when they dominate our lives and are not done within the concept of certain boundaries. They must be made to take their rightful place way down the list. God first in our lives, then our wife or husband and family second, and so on (Cloud & Townsend, pg.129).

> Love not the world, neither the things that are in the world, if any man love the world, the love of the Father is not in him. For all that is in the world, the lust of the flesh, and the lust of the eyes and the pride of life, is not of the Father, but is of this world. And the world is passing away, and the lust thereof. (1 John 2:15, 17)

In our society today where just about anything goes, God does not want us to be chasing whatever pleasure that happens to be the latest fad in this world and to be under the influence of what we see on reality TV shows to the detriment of our spiritual relationship with Him (Greenwood, pg.44). He wants us to be "redeeming the times because the days are evil" (Ephesians 5:16).

As I stated in the first chapter, we're living in a time when no one has been taught or even willing to DENY themselves. To deny oneself nowadays is like a taboo. That is to say that you're not doing you or doing what you feel is best for you. But once again, man was never created to do what he wanted by himself and on his own. Man was created to do what God felt was best for him because man could not see his own end.

Adultery and Fornication

I have given you illustrations of things that you may face to keep you from "denying yourself." However, denying yourself is deeper than not putting God first in your life. Denying yourself has to do with your ability to put God first daily in your life and to make sure that you stop long enough every day to make a conscience choice to choose God. It's not as easy as it sounds and a lot harder than you think. It's easy to deny yourself when you need something from God, but can you deny yourself when what you have been doing for the last few days, weeks, months, or years have convinced you.

For me, it was the workplace. Working my way up the corporate ladder, having to entertain both male and female interest in the company, making alliances, and networking with others as we call it. But a lot of times, when we get to close to others, we can find ourselves committing emotional adultery (Robeson, pg.72) where we become dependent upon talking, speaking, or even being with someone in the name of the job outside of your wife or husband.

The devil is very cunning in this area. It amazes me that normally, you will find someone in the business world that looks great, have a wonderful personality, and dressed well, and by the way, they are going through a rough time with either their significant other or their boyfriend, and they're the person that you have to interact with in order to land the deal or the contract or set up ongoing resources with. Then you already know however business savvy you think you are that you can't handle this kind of interaction. Not because of what's in them but because what you know or don't know that's inside of you.

On the other side of this, we must also be aware that physical adultery and fornication are also the playground for the "Spirit of Whoredoms."

> Now the body is not for fornication, but for the Lord; and the Lord for the body…know ye not that your bodies are the members of Christ? Shall I then take the members of Christ, and make them members of a harlot? God forbids. Flee fornication. Every sin that a man does is without the body; but he that commits fornication sins against his own body. What? Know ye not that your body is the temple of the Holy Ghost which is in you, which ye have of God, and you are not your own? For you are brought with a price: therefore glorify God in your body, and your spirit, which are God's. (1 Corinthians 6:13, 18–20, King James Version, New Life Application Bible)

I want to say this. If you have never received Jesus Christ as your personal Savior and you have a relationship with Him, there is a big possibility that you might not understand the above Scripture. The reason why I say that is you have to be living the Christian life to understand that you can be saved but yet not delivered from doing or committing certain acts against yourself and God. My point in all of this is that if you have truly been Born Again, even though you may have failed miserably in these areas of your life at some point in your life, God will speak to your heart asking you to make a choice of whether you want to continue to do wrong or whether you want to Deny yourself to live right.

Even though extramarital relationships have become the norm in our society, we must understand that God's Word is still the same.

Sexual union outside the marriage bond brings bondage and confusion in our lives that choke out the desire to please God.

In the Book of Hosea, here is the passage context of the phrase in Hosea 1 and 3 in which God uses the prophet's domestic life as an example of God's dealings with Israel: "His union with the nation, her unfaithfulness to the marriage covenant, His chastisement of her, and His love and mercy in redeeming and restoring her to Himself."

Thus, the phrase, under consideration concerning judgment, must be considered in the light of those in the rest of the book which speaks of restoration. The immediate context of the phrase is verse 2–5. Here, the Lord commands Hosea to marry Gomer, an adulterous woman. When a son is born to them, God commanded that his name be called Jezreel. Verses 4 and 5 are the explanation of the prophetic significance of Jezreel's name. This significance is to be found in the history of the several generations preceding Hosea. Ahab and Jezebel, the wicked rulers of Israel, had slain Naboth to obtain his vineyard in Jezreel.

For this, God had pronounced vengeance upon them (I Kings 21). Within approximately fifteen years, this vengeance was executed upon the house of Ahab in Jezreel. Jehu, chosen by God to avenge Naboth's blood upon the house of Ahab, went beyond God's decree and slew a number of other persons at Jezreel (II Kings 9–10). For this reason, God pronounced vengeance upon the house of Jehu for the blood of Jezreel. Hosea uses this vengeance, which was executed upon the descendants of Jehu in his lifetime, to prophesize of a greater vengeance that was to come upon the house of Israel, the Northern Kingdom, and in the house of Ahab in the days of his son (King James), (Connor pg.158).

What must be realized is that no matter how long ago this may have been, if you cannot deny yourself often times when prosperity comes, moral and spiritual degeneration will also come. Secularism and materialism captured the hearts of people just like it does in today's society. Sin runs rampant in our streets today such as swearing, killing, lying, perjury, stealing, adultery, drunkenness, perversion, deceit, oppression, and other things that keep us from denying ourselves. But the thing that grieved the heart of God more than anything else was the sin of idolatry (Hosea 4:12–13; 13:2, KJV). The golden calves set up by Jeroboam about 150 years earlier had opened the floodgates to every evil expression of Canaanite idolatry, including drunkenness, religious prostitution, and human sacrifice.

Since the Lord viewed Israel as His wife, He viewed her worship of other gods as spiritual adultery. The Old Testament speaks frequently of Israel whoring after or playing the harlot with other gods (Deuteronomy 31:16; Judges 2:17, KJV). We too play the harlot mostly in relationships trying to seek the love of someone or somebody to love you right but not realizing whenever purpose is not known, abuse is inevitable. When you do not know the purpose of a thing, you will always abuse yourself. Looking for love in all of the wrong places but yet never being fulfilled because you have never denied yourself and took up your cross and followed God.

Jehovah had told Israel from the beginning that he would not share her with others. Exodus 20:4 says, "You shall not have any other gods before Me." But Israel persistently ignored His command, and by the days of Jeroboam II, the situation was intolerable. God spoke first through the prophet Amos, but the nation of Israel paid little attention. Remember, I said in an earlier chapter that God may have been trying sometimes for years to get your undivided attention for you to deny yourself and follow Him. Such is the case in the Scriptures. So God spoke again. This time, through the prophet Hosea whose name means "Jehovah is salvation."

It was after the birth of Jezreel that Hosea seems to have noticed a change in Gomer. She became restless and unhappy like what some would say a "bird trapped in a cage." Hosea went on preaching and encouraging the wayward nation to turn from their sin and trust God for deliverance from the threat of other nations around them (Bible.Org). REPENTANCE must have been Hosea's theme—return unto the Lord! Hosea preached it repeatedly with power in (Hosea 6:1;14:1). But Gomer seemed less and less interested in his ministry. It even appeared that she may have grown to resent it. I'm sure like most marriages, she felt the weight of Hosea not been home most of the time. She probably accused Hosea of thinking more about his preaching than he did her. Gomer began to find other interests to occupy herself and spent more and more time away from home (Bible.Org).

When a husband and wife have few interests in common, the dangers are great of split up due to the lack of involvement with each other. When this happens, you will soon find that they each have their own set of friends, and there is little communication to bring their two worlds back together because he goes his way, and she goes hers. A husband preoccupation with his work may be the contributing factor to the distance that they now have between them. However, a wife's growing involvement in outside activities and the more she is away from the home, the greater the neglect is. Taking time to do things together as husband and wife will build a unity and a bond that will be an expression of the very work and love of God between them. In this case, Gomer did not share her husband's love for God (Bible.Org).

The Scriptures do not give us the details of what happened, but what it does say would permit us to speculate concerning the progressive trend that led to the tragic situation we eventually are led to discover. Gomer's absences from home grew more frequent and prolonged, and soon, Hosea was feeling pangs of suspicion about her faithfulness to him. He may have laid awake many nights and wrestled with the fears of where Gomer was and what she could be doing. It is probably true that during his daily ministry, he preached with a heavy heart. And his suspicions were confirmed when Gomer got pregnant again. It was a girl this time, and Hosea was convinced that the child was not his. There was no Maury show to go on to get the DNA results. Sometimes, you just know what you know. At God's direction, Hosea called the baby Loruhamah which means "unpitied" or "unloved" implying that she would not enjoy her true father's love. I'm sure that some of you, girls and women, can relate. You may have been born into a bad situation maybe more complicated for you to understand. You may feel unloved, unpitied, and invisible because you desire your father's love. You want to blame you mother, but you recognize that she too was just a product of her environment. She never knew who her father was, so she too has the pains and the scars of being dropped, abandoned, or rejected. Hosea's baby name was symbolic of Israel's wandering from God's love and the discipline she would soon experience. But even the spiritual message could not soothe the prophet's troubled soul (King James Version) (Bible.Org).

No sooner had little Loruhamah been weaned, Gomer conceived again. It was another boy this time. God told Hosea to call him Lo-ammi which meant "not my people" or "no kin of mine." It symbolized Israel's alienation from Jehovah, but it also exposed Gomer's sinful escapades. That child in Hosea's house was not his. I remember after reading this story one day that I heard the Spirit of the Lord speak to my heart and ask me, "How many things have you birth that did not look like Him?"

You see, my friend, when you cannot submit yourself to God as described in James 4:7 and when you cannot deny yourself as described in Matthew 6:24, you will begin to birth things in your life that don't look like God. You will think that God has called you to do a certain work—be it with a certain group of people or even be at a certain church, but if you have not totally sold out to hear the Master's voice and if you have not been qualified by God by going through your test and trials so that God can build character and integrity in you, then you surely will birth things that don't look like God. You will have friends that God did not send to you. You will have a job that God did not ordain for you to be working on. You will have a ministry that you are too immature to handle, and when you began to lose it, all you will do is blame God. But the blame belongs to you because you never got the message that God was and has been calling you to come to the end of yourself.

It was all in the open now. Everyone knew about Gomer's affairs. While the entire second chapter of Hosea's prophecy describes Jehovah's relationship with his unfaithful wife, Israel, it is difficult to escape the feeling that grows out of Hosea's relationship with Gomer sandwiched as it is between two chapters that clearly describe the sad and horrible truth of a story. Hosea pleaded with her (2:2). He threatened to disinherit her (2:3). But still, she ran off with her lovers because they promised lavish material things on her (2:0). He tried to stop her on occasion (2:6), but she continued to seek her companions in sin (2:7). Hosea would take her back in loving forgiveness, and they would try again, but her repentance would be short-lived, and soon, she would be off again with another new lover (King James Version).

Then the time came that Hosea feared the most happened. Gomer was leaving for good this time. She had found her true love, and she was never coming back. How Hosea must have felt. He loved her deeply and grieved for her as though she had been taken in death. His heart must have ached that she would choose a lifestyle that would surely bring her to ruin. His friends probably said, "Good riddance to her. Now you will be through with her adulterous ways once and for all." But Hosea did not feel that way. He longed for her to come home (Bible.Org).

We cannot escape the fact of the message of Hosea's undying love. Hosea wanted to see Gomer restored to his side as his faithful wife. And he believed that God was great enough to do it for him. One day, word came by way of the grapevine gossips that Gomer had been deserted by her lover. She had sold herself into slavery and had hit rock bottom. This was the last straw. Certainly, now Hosea would forget all about her. But his heart said "no." He could not give up on her, and he could not give her up. And then God spoke to him: "Go again, love a woman who is loved by her husband, yet an adulterous, even as the Lord loves the sons of Israel, though they turn to other gods" (Hosea 3:1).

How many times have we turned our backs on God? How many times have we put other people, other things, and other stuff in the place that only God should reside in our lives? Gomer was still beloved by her husband Hosea even though she was an adulterous, and God wanted Hosea to seek her out and prove his love to her. How could anyone love that deeply? The answer would be right there in God's instructions to Hosea: "even as the Lord love." Only one who knows the love and forgiveness of God can ever love this perfectly. And one who has experienced His loving forgiveness cannot help but love and forgive others. Christian husbands are commanded to love their wives as Christ loved the church (Ephesians 5:25), and Hosea is an outstanding biblical example of that kind of love.

Hosea began his search for Gomer driven by his indestructible divine love—a love that bears all things, believes all things, hopes for all things, endures all things, and a love that never ends (I Corinthians 13:7). Hosea found her, and she was ragged, torn, sick, dirty, disheveled, destitute, and chained to an auction block in a filthy slave market—a repulsive shadow of the woman she once was. We wonder how and who could love her now? But Hosea bought her from her slavery for fifteen shekels of silver and thirteen bushels of barley (Hosea 3:2). Then he said to her, "You shall not play the harlot nor shall you have a man. So I will also be toward you" (Hosea 3:3). Hosea actually paid for her, brought her home, and eventually restored her to her position as his wife. While we do not find anything else in Scripture about their relationship with each other, we assume that God used Hosea's supreme act of forgiving love to melt her heart and change her life.

In Hosea 2:16, we read, "And it shall be at that day, saith the Lord that thou shall call me Ishi; and shall call me no more Baali." Ishi, is the Israelite term, in opposition to Baali, the Canaanite term, with the same meaning, though with a significance of its own. Ishi, means my husband and in most circumstances God can be our provider or in this case husband to Israel whom he considered a "tramp."

CHAPTER 5

Breaking the Soul Ties

*Let no one seek his own good, but
the good of his neighbor.*

—1 Corinthians 10:24

The Bible does not specifically talk about "Soul Ties" by using those exact words. However, by researching your Bible, you can understand that Soul Ties can be identified as Strongholds, Yokes, Bondages, Iniquities, Generational Curses, and things that you have permitted to be a part of your Solace Realm.

This next section is of the book I want to share with you comes from research that my spiritual Father and Mother did by Dr. Jerry and Sherill Piscopo with Simon and Trish Presland in their book entitled *Spiritual Warfare*. Let's hear what they have to say about Soul Ties.

Whenever you are in a relationship with someone, whether on a casual basis or a deeper level, soul ties are formed. In its simplest form, a soul tie joins two souls together in the spiritual realm. They bind, fasten, and secure one soul to another. The Bible doesn't use the words "soul tie" but states that we become one flesh with whomever we are joined to.

Soul ties create tendencies and desires within us that can be good or bad. They can pull us toward God or away from him. Consider someone who is born and raised in the church but becomes involved with someone who has no desire for the things of God just like Hosea and Gomer in Chapter 4. More often than not, the Christian will turn away from God rather than the other person choosing a relationship with God. In Hosea's case, it was God's will to show symbolically that God was married to Israel and wanted them to repent and come back to Him just like Hosea wanted Gomer to repent and come back to him, and she did by Hosea buying her back off the auction block displaying the kind of love Christ has for us when He died and paid a debt for us that He did not owe. (Ephesians 2:8–9) says, "For by grace are we saved through faith; and that not of yourselves: it is the gift of God: Verse 9, not of works, lest any man should boast."

Scripture teaches that there are godly soul ties and ungodly ones. Soul ties not only bind two souls together. They unite the spirits and bodies of those involved as well. They can occur in relationships such as those between friends, coworkers, church members, brothers and sisters, parents and children, and husbands and wives. Let's look at a soul tie that develops between a man and a woman as their relationship deepens.

When a man and woman first meet, they primarily relate through words with only superficial connection. If they continue to talk and they decide they like each other, they begin to form a soul tie. There is a connection forming between them that go deeper than what is seen on the surface. When they start to date and share their hopes and dreams, emotions, and future, they deepen their soul tie because they now have an emotional bond. If these people are Christians and they start praying together, they develop a spiritual tie because they are relating on a spiritual level. If this couple chooses to marry, they form a physical tie as they join themselves in a sexual union.

Godly Soul Ties

The Israelites understood that when they entered into "covenant" with someone, they were joining their bodies, souls, and spirits with that person. Covenants can be considered soul ties. Depending on the type of covenant entered into, there can be an exchange of blood, clothing, weaponry, a meal, or names, and/or the participants may build a memorial as a witness to their bond. The Bible contains examples of godly soul ties.

David and Jonathan

We read of a covenant soul tie made between David and Jonathan before David became King of Israel:

"And it came to pass, when he had made an end of speaking unto Saul, that the soul of Jonathan was knit with the soul of David, and Jonathan loved him as his own soul" (I Samuel 18:1).

The words "knit" and "cleave" mean to cling or adhere to and abide (fast) together. When love between two people comes from their hearts, the soul tie between them benefits both parties. Jesus spoke of this kind of love.

"Greater love hath no man than this, that a man lay down his life for his friends" (John 15:13). David and Jonathan exemplified this type of love.

Naomi and Ruth

The book of Ruth gives another example of a godly soul tie. Nomi had lost her husband and both sons while in the country of Moab and wanted to return to her home in Israel. She told both of her daughters-in-law to stay in Moab. Orpah did so, but Ruth said:

> Entreat me not to leave thee, or to return from following after thee: for whither thou goest, I will go; and where thou lodges, I will lodge: thy people shall be my people, and thy God my God: Where thou diest, will I die, and there will be buried: the LORD do so to me, and more also, if ought but death part thee and me. (Ruth 1:16–17)

Naomi and Ruth had spent ten years together. They must have developed a very deep mother-in-law/daughter-in-law soul tie relationship for Ruth to choose to stay with Naomi and forsake her own country.

Marriage

The love Jesus talked about in the Book of John is also the type of soul tie that forms the foundation of a strong and healthy marriage. One that will endure the tests and trails that inevitably come.

"Therefore, shall a man leave his father and his mother, and shall cleave unto his wife: and they shall be one flesh" (Genesis 2:24).

Jesus repeated this on two occasions.

> Two are better than one; because they have a good reward for their labor. For if they fall, the one will lift up his fellow: but woe to him that is alone when he falleth; for he hath not another to help him up. Again, if two lie together, than they have heat: but how can one be warm alone? And if one prevails against him, two shall withstand him; and a threefold cord is not quickly broken. (Ecclesiastes 4:9–12)

The stronger the bond or soul tie between a husband and wife, the longer their relationship will last. The physical, emotional, and mental strengths of one will sustain the other in times of adversity, and they will rejoice together in times of triumph. The Lord highly honors the marriage relationship and the resulting soul ties because it exemplifies his love for the church. Paul relates marriage to the "profound mystery" of Christ's relationship with the church. Thus, we see that God instituted soul ties for the benefit of mankind.

Christ and the Church

The blood Christ shed at Calvary created a soul tie between himself and those who accept his finished work. Christ's blood brought us into right relationship with God. It allows us to be part of his family. We are in a covenant soul tie relationship with him that cannot be broken unless we choose to walk away from him.

Ungodly Soul Ties

Whatever God creates for our benefits and blessing, Satan wants to pervert and curse. This is true of soul ties as well. Ungodly soul ties can form inappropriate male/male, female/female, or male/female relationships through spending too much time together, flirting, or sharing personal struggles—whether at work, church, or other places people interact with.

One of the deepest soul ties we can form comes through sexual union. It involves the bodies, souls, and spirits of those involved. We share our bodies and emotions. Our spirits become united because God created sexual intimacy to be a foundational part of the marriage covenant.

God has designed most women to come under the protection, care, and authority of a man. When a man has sex with her, he sometimes gains a form of dominion over her.

> Unto the woman he said, I will greatly multiply thy sorrow and thy conception; in sorrow, thou shalt bring forth children; and thy desire shall be to thy husband, and he shall rule have dominion over thee. (Genesis 3:16)

Because the sexual relationship between a man and a woman involves body, soul, and spirit, Satan desires to entice and deceive us into sin in this area. Any sexual union (physical, fantasy, or otherwise) that is not with our spouse will always create an ungodly soul tie. The intimate bond formed with another person cannot be blessed by God.

> Ye have heard that it was said by them of old time, Thou shall not commit adultery: But I say

unto you, that whosoever looketh on a woman to lust after her hath committed adultery with her already in his heart. (Matthew 5:27–28)

Paul addressed sexual immorality and the effects it has on us. He points out that we become One Flesh when we have sex with a prostitute (male of female), but this soul tie also extends to anyone we have sex with outside the marriage.

Dinah and Shechem

And Dianah the daughter of Leah, which she bare unto Jacob, went out to see the daughters of the land. And when Shechem the son of Hamor the Hivite, prince of the country, saw her, he took her, and lay with her, and defiled her. And his soul clave unto Dinah the daughter of Jacob, and he loved the damsel, and spoke kindly unto the damsel. (Genesis 34:1–3)

In this story, Shechem, a Hivite, lusted after Dinah, an Israelite, and raped her forming an ungodly soul tie between the two. When Jacob and his sons found out, they were furious and deceived Shechem, his father Hamor, and all males from their city asking them to be circumcised, so the two nations could intermarry (including Shechem and Dinah). Three days into the rite of circumcision, while all the Hivite males were still incapacitated, two of Jacob's sons Levi and Simeon went into the Hivite town and killed all of the men present, including Hamor and Shechem.

Although these consequences are extreme, they represent a sobering point: most sexual involvement outside of marriage will form an ungodly soul tie that can potentially destroy marriages, families, friendships, and even individual lives. God has set into place both natural and spiritual laws that bring either blessing when obeyed or cursing when ignored. Just as marriage forms a godly soul tie that brings blessings, adultery and fornication form ungodly soul ties that invoke bondage and enslavement.

Characteristics of Ungodly Soul Ties

A careful examination of our relationships will reveal godly and ungodly soul ties. We need to ask ourselves. "Does this relationship glorify God? Is it brining me closer to Jesus?"

Just because we have a relationship with another Christian does not necessarily mean there is a godly soul tie formed. Here are some questions to ask ourselves:

- Do you feel you are compromising or being compromised in ways that go against your conscience or God's Word?
- Is the relationship one-sided or self-centered?
- Is there mutual sharing, growth, and freedom? Or is there bondage, control, and manipulation?
- Are the fruits of the Spirit exhibited in the relationship?
- Does the relationship move you toward or away from God?

When impure motives or self-centeredness are at the core of a relationship, the soul tie formed can lead to manipulation and abuse. One person can actually control another through an ungodly soul tie because the minds of the two are open to one another, and the enemy has a legal right to wreak havoc on the relationship.

Breaking Ungodly Soul Ties

Although ungodly soul ties are sinful, the good news is that Jesus forgives all sin. "If we confess our sins, he is faithful and just to forgive us our sins, and to cleanse us from all unrighteousness" (1 John 1:9).

We need to break the unhealthy soul ties we have made with other people regardless of how they were formed. Breaking these is similar to a mother who, after giving birth to her child, allows the umbilical cord that ties the two together to be cut. When this happens, the baby can start its new life and begin to grow on its own. In the same way, it is important that we cut and sever all ungodly ties, so we can move on with our lives. As long as we continue to have ungodly soul ties in our lives, we will not be free to pursue healthy relationships.

Breaking ungodly soul ties involves three important steps: prayer, a willful decision, and walking away. In our personal time with God, we ask him to show us any ungodly relationships we may be involved in. We then ask his forgiveness for our involvement, break and renounce each soul tie formed, and cover them in the blood of Jesus. If we are unsure about particular relationships, talking to a friend you can trust, a pastor, or counselor will help us make a godly decision.

Through acts of our wills, we then mentally choose to leave the ungodly relationships. This is often the hardest part. There has to be an agreement within our wills, or we will not end the relationships. If we are struggling to agree with this, we need to find out what benefits we are receiving by staying in the relationships. As paradoxical as this may sound, even in an abusive relationship, the abused person is benefiting in some way.

Finally we must physically walk away from the ungodly relationships. If possible, we should talk with the other person involved. We should avoid blame but take responsibility for all parts being as honest as possible. The other person may or may not agree, and there may be emotional pain and disappointment involved. However, for our own spiritual growth and peace of mind, we should end the relationships as soon as possible.

> Wherefore come out from among them, and be ye separate, saith the Lord, and touch not the unclean thin; and I will receive you, And will be a father unto you, and ye shall be my sons and daughters, saith the Lord Almighty. (II Corinthians 6:17–18)

When God leads us to break a soul tie, we can trust him to draw us closer to himself in response to our obedience and to help us develop new godly relationships and soul ties (Piscopo, pg.95).

Jesus did not practice "soul healing" in the way we do today because soul healing is simply bringing the presence of Jesus in the hurtful scene and letting Him work. So whenever anyone came into the presence of Jesus when He was living on earth, if they desired it, their soul would be healed as well as their body and spirit (Bennett, pg.52).

To me, God restores your soul as you learn to practice the presence of Jesus in the past as well as in the present and on into the future—helping you to forgive everyone and setting you free to live at your fullest potential (Bennett, pg.49).

CHAPTER 6

Soul Ties, Fingerprints on Your Soul (Revelation)

And those who belong to Christ Jesus have crucified the flesh with its passion and desires.

—Galatians 5:24

In looking at the Bible, James 1:8 tells us that a double-minded man is unstable in all of his ways. That word double-minded in the Greek means *di-psuchos,* meaning "a person with two minds or souls." It's interesting that the word appears only in the Book of James 1:8;4:8. Bible scholars conclude that James might have coined this word. To grasp the full meaning of this word, it is best to understand how it is used within the context.

James writes of the doubting person that he is "like a wave of the sea, blown, and tossed by the wind. "That man should not think that he will receive anything from the Lord; he is a doubleminded man, unstable in all that he does" (James 1:6–8). A Doubter is a double-minded person. Jesus had in mind such a person when He spoke of the one who tries to serve two masters (Matthew 6:24). As such, he is "unstable" which comes from the Greek word that means "unsteady, wavering, in both his character and feelings."

A double-minded person is restless and confused in his thoughts, his actions, and his behavior. Such a person is always in conflict with himself. One torn by such inner conflict can never lean with confidence on God and His gracious promises. Correspondingly, the term unstable is analogous to a drunken man unstable to walk a straight line swaying one way then another. He has no defined direction, and as a result, he doesn't get anywhere. Such a person is "unstable in all he does."

In a recap of the story of Hosea, Hosea 4:6 says, "My people are *destroyed* from a lack of knowledge…"

"And it will be: Like people like Priests" (v 9).

"For the spirit of whoredom has cause to error" (v 12).

1st Thessalonians 4:3 says that it is God's will that we should be sanctified, but the problem with people today is that they are so messed up in their solace realm that they cannot push through to be blessed. They refuse to Deny themselves of worldly pleasure, and their sin causes them to error. In some cases, people today find themselves giving themselves away to others in sexual sin, and when they have sex with someone, you pass on to them a spiritually connection that whatever spirits they had, you now have it as well because you have allowed someone else to occupy a place in your Soul that only God, your husband or wife was supposed to be, and now you're connected to that person. And you wonder why they can treat you wrong, but you can't get over them. It's because they are in your solace realm, and now you have a fingerprint on your soul which is a soul tie because you refused to deny yourself.

God didn't want us fornicating and not having sex because he was trying to be cruel to us. God knew that whomever we have sex with, they become a part of us. Psychologists have said that whomever you have sex with means that you have just shared every partner that they or you have ever had. Every time you have sex with someone, especially out of wedlock, you leave and they leave a piece of themselves with you because it is a transfer of spirits—fingerprints on your soul.

That is why James is stressing the fact that a double-minded person is unstable in all of their ways. That word double-minded in the Greek meaning *di-psuchos*. Di means Two while Psuchos means Soul in which where we get our root word Psycho which Webster dictionary defines as someone who is mentally unstable or afflicted with a psychosis: a person filled with delusions and hallucinations that occur in the absence of insight. We also get another word from the word double-minded, and that's Schizo which is where we get the word schizophrenia from which according to Webster's dictionary, it means having a form of psychosis marked by a strong tendency to dissociate oneself from reality. Schizophrenia is often characterized by hallucinations, delusions, and inappropriate reactions to situations. The word schizophrenia is often used informally as well as scientifically to indicate a split personality. You may ask, what does this have to do with me? Well, I'm glad you asked. When you don't deny yourself, you become what you do. So if you're having sex with someone and they are not your husband or your wife—I'm talking about a man with woman as wife and husband—you create a Soul Tie that allows the other person to become a part of you in your solace realm where only God and your husband or wife is supposed to reside.

So then because they are not your wife or husband and, in a lot of cases, it was only a "booty call" or he/she was just someone you causally have sex with, the closer you all are together and the more frequent you spend time with them, you can develop inappropriate reactions to situations where you begin to act like husband and wife, argue like husband and wife, and, in some cases, have bank accounts together, live together, and have kids together but never marry but can't stop being with this person in some capacity all because you have a soul tie.

And when they make you mad, you find yourself acting like they're yours. And, in extreme cases, they may even be married to someone else, but you can't let go because you are double-minded and have a split soul. In the soul are the will, emotions, and the intellect (mind). When you yield your spirit to whoredom, you don't realize what happens to you. When you do, you'd think you just went to bed with someone. You think you just got weak. You think you can do a little something and repent about it later and go on with your life. But what you don't realize is when you hit it, you split it. You become double-minded—two souls; split soul.

You develop a Dr. Jekyll, Mr. Hide mentality, and that's on a nature level. On a spiritual level, whenever someone has two souls, they cannot be true to the move of God. In our Spirit, we are God conscience. In our Soul, we are self-conscience. And in our body, we are sense conscience.

God spoke this same truth to Abraham in Genesis 17:9 when God said unto Abraham, "Thou shall keep my covenant therefore thou, and they seed after thee in their generations."

"This is my covenant, which ye shall keep, between me and you and they seed after thee; every man child among you shall be circumcised" (v 10).

"And ye shall circumcise the flesh of your foreskin; and it shall be a token of the covenant between me and you (blood Covenant)" (v 11).

"And he that is eight days old shall be circumcised among you, every man child in your generations, he that is born in the house, or bought with money or any stranger, which is not of thy seed" (v 12).

"He that is born in thy house, and he that is bought with thy money, must needs be circumcised; and the *covenant shall be in your flesh for an everlasting covenant*" (v 13).

In essence, what God was saying is this, if I can get you to control your private part, then I can control you and bless you, and multiply you, and make your name great (Genesis 17:9–13, KJV).

Sex of itself is good. It is a gift from God. It's for procreation, consummate, and recreation. The Bible says that Isaac was sporting with his wife. Getting together with his wife or your husband is not just a physical thing or a release, but it's a renewal of a covenant. A lot of people cannot understand why they are saved, but their marriages are messed up. When purpose is not known, abuse is inevitable. If you understand the principle, it brings you to another level. When you understand it, you will appreciate it. But anything you don't understand, you'll look at it differently. A girl looks at it as giving herself to a guy, and the guy looks at it totally differently as conquering the girl. Anything you conquer, you consider your property—his territory. But what he does not realize is that in conquering her, he just lost himself and devalues her.

Many people get healed in their bodies or their spirit but not in their souls. The Bible says that God prayed that your spirit, soul, and body be found blameless. Revelation 17:18 says that the battle is over your soul. Jesus said, "What profits a man to gain the whole world and lose his soul or what shall a man give in exchange for his soul" (Matthew 6:24, KJV). You don't lose your soul gradually when you have sex outside of the marriage that God intended for us to have. You lose your soul immediately.

In life, things can happen that can mess your intellect or your will or your emotions up so that you can lose your soul immediately. What you feel and what you want can mess you up if it's not for the right reason and with the right intent. Your solace realm can be so messed up that what you think is what you do. The Bible says, "So as a man thinks in his heart, so is he." If you think sex, sex, sex, sex all day or drinking, drinking, drinking, you become indicative of you charter. You solidify the curse that is working in you all because you can't Deny yourself.

Jeremiah 8: 29 tell us that the harvest is past, the summer is ended, and we are not saved. Like I said to you in Chapter 1, how many signs does God need to give you for you to take your track shoes off from running from Him and allow Him to take control over your life? Every year and every New Year's Eve, you promised yourself that you were going to do better, start over, turn over a new leaf, let negative people go, and get right with God and go to church. You make a good go at it, but yet you still find yourself right back in what you said you weren't going to do again. You have what the Book of Jeremiah says is a slight healing. Jeremiah 8:11 says, "For they have healed the hurt of the daughter of my people slightly, saying Peace, peace; when there is no peace."

You go to church having service but not healed. When you do get healed, it's only a partial of healing. Your body won't take you anywhere that your mind has not already been. So what you think you are is what you are. So if your intellect is in your solace realm then what you think is what you do. So if sin has affected your soul through your emotions, will, and intellect, then you can't do right.

> For we know that the law is spiritual: but I am carnal, sold under sin. Verse 15, for that which I do allow not: for what I would, that do I not; but what I hate, that do I.
>
> If then I do that which I would not, I consent unto the law that is good. Now then it is no more I that do it, but sin that dwells in me. For I know that in me (that is in my flesh,) dwells no good thing: for to will is present with me; but how to perform that which is good I find not. For the good that I would I do not; but the evil which I would not, that I do. Now if I do that I would not, it is no more I that do it, but sin that dwells in me. I find then a law, that, when I would do good, evil is present with me. For I delight in the law of God after the inward man. But I see another law in my members, warring against the law of my mind, and brining me into captivity to the law of sin which is in my members.
>
> O wretched man that I am! Who shall deliver me from the body of this death? I thank God through Jesus Christ or Lord. So then with the mind I myself serve the law of God' but with the flesh the law of sin. (Romans 7:14–25, KJV)

Solomon said that he loved God, but he sacrifice in the high places and bow down unto idols. How can we say we love God, yet do the things that we do to God? The Bible says that Solomon's wives turn his heart away from God (1 Kings 11:4).

Let's take a look now at the story of David's seduction of Bathsheba as told in 2 Samuel 11. The story is told that David, while walking on the roof of his palace, saw Bathsheba, who was then the wife of Uriah, having a bath. He immediately desired her and later made her pregnant (2 Samuel 11:1).

The story concerns David, the greatest hero of Hebrew History, and by God's testimony, a man after His own heart (Samuel 13:14; Acts 13:22). But men have weakness and even men after God's own heart. And God is not ashamed to share with us the weaknesses of His greatest saints. We learn some indispensable lessons from their mistakes such as the utter vileness of our hearts, the horrible consequences of our sin, and the unfathomable depts. Of God's forgiving grace, so let us learn from David.

David was somewhere in his forties now. The vulnerable age, they tell us. He had accomplished some remarkable military feats—extending the borders of Israel and securing them against every major surrounding nation. He owed himself a rest, or so he thought, and that is where the story begins. And we read in 2 Samuel 11 which says:

> In the spring, at the time when kings go off to war, during this time period kings went out to battle in the spring because the winter months curtailed the movement of the troops. David sent Joab out with the king's men and the whole Israelite army. They destroyed the Ammonites and besieged Rabbah. But David remained in Jerusalem.
>
> One evening David got up from his bed and walked around on the roof of the palace. From the roof, he saw a woman bathing. The woman was very beautiful, and David sent someone to find out about her. The man said she is Bathsheba, the daughter of Eliam and the wife of Uriah the Hittite. Then David sent messengers to get her. She came to him and he slept with her. (Now she was purifying herself from her monthly uncleanness.) Then she went back home. The woman conceived and sent word to David, saying I am pregnant. (2 Samuel 11:1–5)

Being tempted is no sin. It's the yielding to the temptation that's the sin—lingering over it, toying with it, and flirting with it. That's where we fall into sin. We can tantalize ourselves to such a degree that resisting the sin is no longer considered to be a possible option. The only question that remains is how we are going to do it. God says that we should flee temptation (II Timothy 2:22). And he will help us handle it if we obey. But if we waddle and play around with sin, we are doomed to fall in it sooner than later. When a man finds himself attracted to a woman, for example, and either one of them are married, he needs to get himself out of that situation quickly. The longer he nurtures the relationship, the harder it will be to break it off until ultimately, he will hear himself saying stupid things like "But I just can't live without her." And before he realizes the implications of what he is saying, his life and family will be in shambles.

Bathsheba is not guiltless either. She may not have purposely enticed David, but she was immodest and indiscreet. To disrobe and bathe in an open courtyard in full view of any number of rooftops patios in the neighborhood was asking for trouble. She could have easily have bathed indoors. Even so in our day, some women do not seem to realize what the sight of their flesh can do to a man. They allow themselves to be pushed into the fashion mold of the world and wear revealing cloths or nearly nothing. Then they wonder why the men they meet cannot think of anything but sex. We must not fail to instruct our young girls in these matters, particularly as they enter their teen years. Christian parents should teach their daughters facts about the nature of man and the meaning of modesty, and then agree on standards for their dress (King James Version) (Bible.Org).

David found out who the beautiful young bather was and sent for her, and the thought became the deed. There is no evidence that this was a forcible rape. Bathsheba seems to have been a willing partner. Her husband was off to war, and she was lonely. The glamor of being desired by the attractive king meant more to her than her commitment to her husband and her dedication to God. They probably cherished those moments together. Maybe they even assured themselves that it was a tender and beautiful experience. Most times, we do. Your body has a central nervous system for every eighteen feet of skin. You have blood vessels. You have approximately seventy-two feet of nerves. When your skin is touched, it sends a message to your brain, and the censor in your brain relays what you feel. This is why when you have sex with someone, you become knitted with them because your body becomes their body and your spirit their spirit and their soul your soul. Any time after you have been touched, turn on, excited, or stimulated by someone, that feeling has left a blueprint on your sensor memory which means that you now have fingerprints on your soul.

In God's eyes, what David and Bathsheba had done was ugly and hideous. Satan had baited his trap, and they were now in his clutches. They would both soon find out just how much hell they really were in (Bible.Org).

David gets word that Bathsheba is now pregnant, this was a crisis in that culture, for it would have meant death by stoning according to the Law of Moses (Leviticus 20:10). What would people think if this got out? Would they think that Bathsheba was a tramp and David was a hoe? No, not the King. But yet in still in our society today, this is what we call Reality TV. There is nothing new under the sun (Ecclesiastes 1:9).

No crisis had ever shaken David before, and he was certainly not going to let this one destroy him either. David devised a plan to bring Bathsheba's husband (Boo) home from the battle for a few days. Then her husband would surely have sex with his wife while he is home, and nobody would ever know that she is pregnant and the baby is his. But Uriah Bathsheba's husband was too patriotic to enjoy his wife while his fellow soldiers' lives were still in danger on the battlefield, so he slept in the barracks with the king's servants. Then David had to put plan *B* into action. How many of you know that sin you will have putting plans *A* through *Z* into place if it means you getting out of the mess you created for you?

David calmly wrote Uriah's death warrant, sealed it, and sent it to Joab saying, "Put Uriah on the front lines, and when the enemy comes toward him, have your men pull back so that he, Uriah, would be killed."

Now murder was added to David's account all because of an ungodly soul tie of adultery. After a short period time of mourning, Bathsheba entered David's house and became his wife, and the two lovers are finally together and free to be with each other to enjoy freely and uninterruptedly—except for one thing: "But the thing that David done was evil in the sight of the Lord" (II Samuel 11:27).

David knew he had sinned. Most of the time we usually do. If not on the surface, deep down in us, we know it was wrong what we did. But like David, we try to ignore it. We try to go on living life like it never happened. If David's conscience got too heavy, he could always rationalize by saying things like, "I'm the King. I can do as I please. It really was Bathsheba's fault for tempting me anyway. Besides, who am I hurting? Men die in battle all the time. This is war!"

The possibilities available to help us excuse our sin are endless. But there was something gnawing at David in the pit of his stomach, an emptiness he could not describe accompanied by periods of extreme depression. Yes, there are feelings from doing wrong that we can carry with us every day. That's the feeling that Satan wants us to carry with us because it keeps us in debt to him so that we can't really move on. Feelings of guilt, shame, fear, abandonment, and rejection just to name a few are all feelings that can keep you stagnated and stuck in a rut for years if you let it. Let's see what happens next in the story.

He later wrote three Psalms describing those months being out of fellowship with God: Psalms 32, 38, and 51. Listen to the cry of David in the Psalm:

"I am bent over and greatly bowed down; I go mourning all day long. I am benumbed and badly crushed; I groan because of the agitation of my heart" (Psalm 38:6–8).

David loved the Lord and tried to worship him, but he found a barrier there. It is the barrier of his own sin. What the enemy never tells you while you think that you are enjoying yourself in sin is that your sin will cut you off from the presence and fellowship with God. God seemed far from David. He wrote: "Do not forsake me, O Lord;

O my God, do not be far from me!" (Psalm 38:21). His friends sensed his irritability and avoided him:

My loved ones and my friends stand aloof from my plague; and my kinsmen stand afar off" (Psalm 38:11). David lived that way for nearly a year. He had his precious Bathsheba, but he had no rest for his soul (King James Version) (Bible.Org).

As I'm writing this, I can remember times that I was so far from God not knowing if I could ever get back in right standing with him. I was saved in my spirit but struggle and failing miserable in my body and solace realm with no one to talk to because if I go to the church, they will judge me. If I go to my family, they will talk about me. If I go to my friends, they will despise me. When you can't turn to the world for hope, just know no matter how bad or big the problem seems, God is BIGGER, and He is waiting for you to REPENT and DENY yourself and to return back home to Him. He's waiting for you. Let's stop here for a moment of prayer:

> Father,
>
> I confess my sins to you right now: sins of omission, sins of commission, sins I see, and sins I don't see. Blot out my transgressions, and cleanse me from all sin. I Repent right know, God, and I acknowledge to you that I don't know the way. I don't know how to take care of me. I ask that you become my God as you always was, but I surrender my will to do as you say. All of the people I hurt and all of those that hurt me, I forgive. Please, God, forgive me. Take me back to the place in my soul where I first fell in love with you. I thank you for your mercy and your grace. Send healing for my life. In Jesus's name I pray. AMEN!

One Day, God sent the prophet Nathan to David with a very interesting story: Nathan began to say, "There were two men in one city, the one rich and the other poor. The rich man had a great many flocks and herds. But the poor man had nothing except one little lamb which he brought and nourished, and it grew up together with him and his children. It would eat of his bread and drink of his cup and lie in his bosom and was like a daughter to him. Now a traveler came to the rich man, and he was unwilling to take from his own flock or his own herd to prepare for the wayfarer who had come to him; rather he took the poor man's lamb and prepared it for the man who had come to him" (2 Samuel 12:1–4). When David heard the story, he was furious at this rich man's selfish insensitivity and insisted that he deserved to die.

Guilt is a cold piece to deal with. It often caused us to lash out harshly and severely at the sins of others when we have the most to hide ourselves. What we have hidden inside of us erupts against them. I'm sure it was with fear and trembling that Nathan uttered his next words. Other men had lost their heads for saying less than this to kings, but he was bound by his calling to deliver the message of God to the erring king.

He pointed his convicting finger at David and said, "You are the man!" Then he delivered the message that God would have him to say to David:

> It is I who anointed you King over Israel and it is I who delivered you from the hand of Saul. I also gave you your master's house, and your master's wives into you care, and I gave you the house of Judah; and if that had been too little, I would have added many more things like these. Why have you despised the word of the Lord by doing evil in His sight? You have struck down Uriah the Hittie with the sword, have taken his wife to be your wife, and have killed him with the sword of the sons of Ammon. (2 Samuel 12:7–9)

And the conviction of God's Spirit penetrated the depths of David's soul. Here it is a year later, and David's sins finally caught up with him. That's exactly how it happens. When you least expect it, you are faced to deal with the sins of your past and present. Sin leaves us with unhappy consequences, and God does not always see fit to eliminate them. He knows that experiencing the effects of our sin will help us become more sensitive to His will. The consequences of David's sin would be far-reaching and long lasting. First the sword would never depart from his house (2 Samuel 12:10).

The people in the palace knew it. David's son Absalom knew it. And when he killed his half-brother Amnon for rapping his sister (II Samuel 13:28). He probably justified his actions by thinking, "Dad did it. So why can't I?"

Joab knew it. He was the one who carried out David plan to kill Uriah. And he probably used it to excuse himself when he murdered Absalom (II Samuel 18:14) and later Absalom's captain, Amasa (2 Samuel 20:9–10). The sword never did depart from David's house. Our sin affects those closest to us most of the time (Bible Hub, Articles).

Secondly, David's sin would rise up evil against him out of his own house (2 Samuel 12:11). Thirdly, David's wives would be taken before his eyes and given to someone else who would be with them in broad daylight (2 Samuel 12:11), (2 Samuel 16:22). Fourth, the child born of David's illicit affair with Bathsheba would die (II Samuel 12:14). That baby would give the enemies of God cause to blaspheme, so God graciously took the child home to Himself.

Did you notice why God took the baby? It was because by David's deed had "given occasion to the enemies of the Lord to blaspheme." Now we understand one important reason for divine discipline. It is administered, so the enemies of God will know that He is Infinitely Holy and Righteous that God will deal with sin even in His children. David had to bear the consequences of his sin and so must we. That burden can be heavy, but the time to think about that is before we yield (Bible Hub, Article).

It all comes back to denying ourselves and doing things in God's way because our way just doesn't work apart from God. David says in Psalm 51:

> Have mercy upon me, O God, according to thy lovingkindness: according unto the multitude

> of thy tender mercies blot out my transgression. Wash me thoroughly from mine iniquity, and cleanse me from my sin. For I acknowledge my transgressions: and my sin is ever before me. Against thee, thee only, have I sinned, and done this evil in thy sight: that thou might be justified when thou speak, and be clear when thou judge. Behold, I was shape in iniquity, and in sin did my mother conceive me. Behold thou desires truth in the inward parts: and in the hidden part thou shalt make me to know wisdom. Purge me with hyssop (truth), and I shall be clean: wash me, and I shall be whiter than snow. (Psalm 51:1–7)

David finally realized here in the Scriptures that everything he had done and everything that was said, God saw his every deed and knew in His heart that it was evil. We, as saints, have to be careful not to believe the lie that the enemy normally tells us when we have done something against God, and that lie is: "Go ahead and do it. God will forgive you. God knows your heart."

Here's the problem with sin. After committing it, you're not guaranteed that you can make it back from the deeds that you have done. We have to live in the flesh, so I am aware that as long as we are in the flesh, we will sin. But there is a difference from falling into sin and waddling in it. There is a difference from committing a sinful act maybe not as devastating as David's sin but sin all the same. Practicing sin means you do it every day, and you wear it on you like a scarf or a hat. They use the term "God knows my heart." He really does, and he knows that you are a dangerous person because the heart is deceitful above all things, and desperately wicked: who can know it? (Jeremiah 17:9)

In Psalm 51:10–12, David went on and said: "Create in me a clean heart, O God, and renew a right spirit in me. Cast me not away from thy presence; and take not thy holy spirit from me. Restore unto me the joy of thy salvation; and uphold me with thy free spirit."

Some of David's closing remarks in this chapter are seen in verse 17, "the sacrifices of God are a broken spirit: a broken and a contrite heart, O God, thou will not despise."

David's plea for mercy, forgiveness, and cleansing was made unto God all because He did not DENY himself from the beginning.

I would be remised if I did not share with you something that tells us that David had an ungodly soul tie, and we can find this in the Scriptures in Psalm 23. Psalm 23 is probably one of the most remembered and rehearsed, talked about, and used Psalm in the Bible. However, it holds an infallible truth, and that is verse 1, "the Lord is our shepherd, we shall not lack."

"He makes us to lie down in green pastures; he leads us beside the still waters" (v 2).

David says, "He restores my soul" (v 3), which means he must have lost it at some time or another? Sin will cause you to eventually lose your soul, lose your love for God, and lose your identity in God.

When we allow God, our shepherd, to guide us, we have contentment. When we choose to sin, however, we go our way and cannot blame God for the environment we create for ourselves. Our shepherd knows "the green pastures" and "still waters that will restore us." We will reach these places only by denying ourselves and following him obediently. Rebelling against the shepherd's leading is actually rebelling against our own best interests. We must remember this the next time we are tempted to go our way rather the shepherd's way. Our way ends with guilt and shame. Jesus is the true vine, and God the Father is the husbandman.

> Every branch in Jesus that bears not fruit he takes away: and every branch that bears fruit, he purgeth it, that it may bring forth more fruit. Now ye are clean through the word which I have spoken unto you. Abide in me, and I in you. As the branch cannot bear fruit of itself, except it abide in the vine, no more can ye, except ye abide in me. I am the vine, ye are the branches: He that abides in me, and I in him, the same brings forth

much fruit: for without me ye can do nothing. There is the key people "without God we can do nothing." (John 15:1–5)

For most people, it seems like they can do whatever they want to do and get away with it, or so it seems. When it comes to you and I, we always get caught or caught up. It could be because God has his hands on you and over your life. No matter what you have done and is doing right now, He knows what's best for you.

Chapter 7

Getting Your Soul Back

If any man is to come after me, let him deny himself, take up his cross and follow me.

—Matthew 16:24

We must clearly understand the call that Jesus has placed on our lives. Like Paul, when he was called by God, his conversion on the Damascus road was one in which he did not have to consult another man to determine whether or not he had been called by God. But before he was released to begin his ministry and his mission, Paul went to Abrabia for three years. Why did Paul go to Arabia for three years before he ever met another disciple of Jesus Christ? The Scripture does not tell us plainly why Paul spent three years in Arabia. However, based upon many examples of God placing special calls on people's lives, we know it often requires a time to develop an intimate knowledge and relationship with the newfound Savior. His life was about to change dramatically. That is why you are not what you have been through, and you are not what you're going through right now. The anointing on your life outweighs the hell you may be experiencing in your life right now.

So often when God has placed a call on your life, it requires separation between the old life and the new life. There is a time of being away from the old in order to prepare the heart for what is to come. It can be a painful and difficult separation. Joseph was separated from his family. Jacob was sent to live with his uncle Laban. Moses was sent to the desert.

I believe that in order for God to do a deeper work in our lives, it requires a separation from all we have known before. We have to get our soul back. God is removing all that confidence we place in ourselves up to this point. For me, this time has been very painful and very scary since I am approaching my early to mid-fifties. In my mind, I knew God was calling me to a higher place, and now that He has done that, everything is new. I'm starting over again. God has removed all my comfort zones and securities and crutches in order to accomplish a much greater work in my life that I could not see.

And so it is with you, my friend. People are not your enemy. Sometimes, we look at people because of their attitude toward us, and we determine that they are the reason why things are not going the way we would like them to go in our lives. But I have come to realize that people don't have the power to stop the move of God in my life or yours. People may be used by the devil, but people can't stop the hand of God that has ordained blessing upon your life. My fight and our fight are with the enemy. He does not want us to learn the lessons that are being taught to us by God. The enemy is intimated not because of who you are but because of who you're becoming.

In Jude 1:3, Jude writes: "Beloved, while I was very diligent to write to you concerning our common salvation, I found it necessary to write to you exhorting you to contend earnestly for the faith which was once delivered to the saints." Jude's initial desire was to write about our common salvation. But something happened. Jude found it necessary to write a different letter. We might say that this was the letter that didn't want to be written. The letter of Jude is essentially a sermon. It is Jude preaching against the dangerous practices and doctrines that put the Gospel of Jesus Christ in peril. There were serious issues, and Jude dealt with them seriously (Wiersbe, p 843).

We can be thankful that Jude was sensitive to the Holy Spirit because otherwise, we might have only been receiving a letter from a Christian leader to a particular church instead of this letter becoming a precious instrument inspired by the Holy Spirit and valuable as a warning in these last days.

The point here is that Jude was describing us as "those who are called, loved in God the Father, and kept for Jesus Christ." God calls, God loves, and God keeps. However, Jude shows us the dangers that are around us. This is not the time to die but to live. There is a faith once for all delivered to the saints to rise up and be the men and women that God has called us to be. This faith is worth contending for. This faith is repeatedly threatened from within the church, and we have to fight the good fight of Faith. Every genuine believer should contend to fight for the faith. Sometimes, the word faith is used for the feeling of trust in Jesus. Other times as it is here, it is used for the truths we believe about the one we trust. Christianity is primarily a relationship with God through Jesus Christ, His Son, rather than a set of ideas. No one is saved by believing a set of ideas. We are saved by hope in God through Jesus Christ. Unless a person has a living trust in Jesus as Savior and Lord, all of your righteousness is as filthy rags.

We, as the people of God, must be aware of some very important facts: We should earnestly contend for the faith which was once delivered unto the saints. "We must be ye steadfast, unmovable, always abounding in the work of the Lord, for as much as you know that your labor is not in vain in the Lord" (1 Corinthians 15:58, King James Version). Know that there are certain men who crept in unawares. As leaders, we must start protecting the sheep and not allow everything to come into our pulpits. We must watch as well as pray. We have to seek the mind of God in everything that we do by being sensitive to the spirit of God. 1st Peter 5:2 says, "Taking oversight thereof, not by constraint, but willingly, not for filthy lucre, but of a ready mind. The love of money is the root to all evil."

Are we doing it, whatever it may be, for money? Or are we doing "it" for Christ? Being examples to the flock, stop going after strange flesh. Jude 1:7 says, "For there shall be mockers in the last time, who should walk after their own ungodly lust." We must keep ourselves in the love of God, looking for mercy of our Lord Jesus Christ unto eternal life. We must return back to our place in God in teaching others the lessons that we have learned so that they too can stop living in sin. We must stand up for the Gospel and the plan of salvation and tell people what they must do to be saved. Stop dressing it up. The sinner's prayer is a step in salvation. We must prepare people to meet their God by preaching Holiness and by not having a double standard. We must teach our young people to apply God's Word to their very lives for God has no respect of persons. But our young people must repent! Stop and turn around. Our youth is our future and the future church. So we must earnestly contend (strive) for the faith, which was once delivered unto the saints. The faith is ours.

STUDY READING

> "Thou therefore endure hardness, as a good solider of Jesus Christ. No man that warreth entangled himself with the affairs of this life; that he may please him who has chosen him to be a solider. And if any man also strive (contend) for masteries, yet is he not crowned; except he strive (contend) lawfully. The husbandman that laboureth must be first partaker of the fruits. Consider what I say; and the Lord give thee understanding in all things. For the time will come when they will not endure sound doctrine; but after their own lust shall they heap to themselves teacher, having itching ears; and shall turn away their ears from the truth, and shall be turned unto fables. But watch thou in all things, endure afflictions, do the work of an evangelist, make full proof of thy ministry. (2 Timothy 2:3–7)

We must continue to strive for the faith which was once delivered to the saints. Paul stated after fighting for the Gospel, "I have fought the good fight, I have finished my course, I have kept the faith" (2 Timothy 4:6–7).

Are we keeping the faith? Are we fighting the good fight of faith? Believe me. It's worth fighting for. The apostle treaded the way. Yes, things are bad, but that gives us even more reason to contend, taking a stand for truth and enduring hardness as a good Soldier of Jesus Christ. Jude is a very short book, but it will enlighten us on the conditions that are presently in our midst today. But Jude, the brother of James and the servant of Jesus Christ, states:

> Now unto him that is able to keep you from falling, and to present you faultless before the presence of his glory with exceeding joy. To the only wise God, our Savior, be glory and majesty, dominion and power, both now and forever.

God is able to keep us. God is able to protect. He is the only wise God. He has power, if we got to fight. We must fight the good fight of faith, laying hold on eternal life (Guthery, p 72).

We have got to get our souls back. Looking back at David, the prophet Nathan's penetrating words of exposure of David's sin and his powerful exposition of God's righteousness brings David to his knees, acknowledging his sins: "I have sinned against the Lord," he cried (2 Samuel 12:13).

These were the words God wanted to hear, and they are the words that God wants to hear from us as well. David's spirit was broken; his heart was contrite (Psalms 51:17). And as a result, he heard the sweetest, most pleasant, most beautiful, and most assuring words known to man: "The Lord also has taken away your sin" (2 Samuel 12:13). As David put it in the Psalms, "I acknowledged my sin to Thee, and my iniquity I did not hide; I said, 'I will confess my transgressions to the Lord'; and thou didst forgive the guilt of my sin" (Psalm 32:5).

First John 1:9 tells us, "If we confess our sins, he is faithful and just to forgive us of our sins and to cleanse us from all unrighteousness." That's how you get your soul back—you repent, confess your sins to the Lord, and ask Him to cleanse you, then you will discover the fear of the Lord again. People don't change because they see the light. People change when they feel the heat of God's wrath.

In essence, God is saving you from Himself: His judgment and His wrath. The Bible clearly states that "the wages of sin is death but, the gift from God is eternal life, through Jesus Christ our Lord" (Romans 6:23). Galatians 6:7–9 tells us, "do not be deceived: God is not mocked for whatsoever a man soweth, that shall he also reap." You eventually have to face up to the consequences of your actions. We have to learn how to do what Jeremiah 8:20 says, "The harvest is past, the summer is ended, and we are not saved."

Every year, we may say to ourselves that we are going to do better only to find ourselves sitting in the same defeat that we have always been in year after year. I call them Merry Go Round Test, but in reality, they are iniquities that I spoke on earlier. Iniquities are weakness in our flesh be it our character, our bodies, or our soul that causes us to continually fail to stand fast in the liberty where Christ has made us free. We continue to go back and forth in and out of sin (spiritual scuba diving) in and out of test that we should have been delivered from or should have let go of by now, but we have yet to learn how to let go of the spiritual strongholds that cause us to be bound.

> (Jeremiah 8:21–22) Goes on to say for the hurt of the daughter of my people am I hurt; I am black; astonishment hath taken hold of me. Is there no balm in Gilead; is there no physician there? Why then is not the health of the daughter of my people recovered.

I'll tell you why God's people have not recovered from their sins, and we will talk about it in the next chapter. It's because people today have a case of the "I can't help it." People today are more focus on looking at what others do to them than what they do to people and themselves.

Jeremiah 8:11 tells us what's really wrong with the people. The Scriptures say, "For they have healed the hurt of the daughter of my people slightly, saying, Peace, peace, when there is no peace." We come to church, we clap our hands, stomp our feet, dance, shout, praise, and worship, but when we go home, we don't change. I told you before that the devil don't mine if you come to church. He only mines when you change. So God's people, including me at one time, hold positions in the church. Prophet this, apostle that, or maybe you're just a lay member and have no title or position, but you still belong to God. We have these titles but are hurting and broken and are healed but only slightly, so we spend years in position and years of being in relationship with God but never entering into "fellowship" with Him. Saved but still drinking, saved but still sexing, saved but still cursing, and saved but ready when someone make you mad to put your Holy Ghost on the shelf and have your salvation put on probation because someone made you mad.

We have never learned how to get over ourselves. You are not all that! Get over it. God called us to love one another. You can't do that if your Holy Ghost is on the shelf. The answer, my friend, is that you got to dig up the bones. Jeremiah 8:1–2 tells us this at the time when you begin to deny yourself:

> Saith the Lord, "They shall bring out the bones of the kings of Judah, and the bones of his princes, and the bones of the priests, and the bones on the prophets, and the bones of the inhabitants of Jerusalem, out of their graves. And they shall spread them before the sun, and the moon, and all the host of heaven, whom they have loved, and whom they have served, and after whom they have walked, and whom they have sought, and whom they have worshipped: they shall not be gathered, nor be buried; they shall be for dung upon the face of the earth."

What God was saying to the people here is the threat that the graves of Judah's people would be opened, which was horrible to the people that highly honored the dead and believed it is the highest insult to open graves. This would be an ironic punishment for idol worshipers. Their bodies would be laid out before the sun, moon, stars, and the gods they thought could save them.

For us, it means like Israel. How many things you think you're going to keep putting before God? Our jobs, our relationships, our families, and other pleasures. You are always putting God on the back burner and getting to him either when you feel like it or when trouble comes in your life. You cry out to God for help. But the reality is, God is saying that you got to dig up the bones of everyone that hurt you and everyone you hurt. In some cases, you need to call or send a text or a letter or talk with them personally, to someone you hurt, telling them that you were wrong for your part in whatever causes you to part ways or hurt them or be hurt by them.

It's okay to apologize. It's okay to be godly and be sorry for what you have done. It's called REPENTANCE and FORGIVENESS. Because as you repent by laying the bones out, notice the Scripture says things like dung, mess, and refuge before the sun and moon. All you need is a little rain when you have mess and sun. It makes fertilizer. The things that hurt you and the things that you've done to hurt others when you repent get it right turnaround. Repent unto the Lord and stop doing what you want to do. God will make all of your failures and past hurts be fertilizer in your life that will bring you growth. Someone once said that I never would have made it without God, but I'm stronger, wiser, and better because of what I went through. The Scripture puts it this way, "And we know all things work together for good to them that love God, to them who are called according to his purpose" (Romans 8:28). Isn't that wonderful news? No matter what we have done or what we are doing—good or bad, if we get our hearts right with God, He will even make our bad work out together for our good. What a mighty God we serve! It's time to get your soul back!

CHAPTER 8

Breaking the Chain of the "I Can't Help Its"

For the one who sows to his own flesh will from the flesh reap corruption, but the one who sows to the Spirit will from the Spirit reap eternal life.

—Galatians 6:8

People's past hinders them from receiving God's salvation. The past can hinder deliverance. The past can have a stronghold on an individual's life, therefore, preventing their future from reaching the full potential that God intended. The past can hinder growth of development. "Therefore, if any man be in Christ, he is a new creature; old things are passed away, behold all things are become new" (2 Corinthians 5:17). The **Old** things must pass away:

- Old relationships
- Old friends
- Old ways of thinking
- Old attitudes
- Old places

The past hinders one from giving acceptable sacrifice. In order to live in Christ, we must die out to the world. Trying to hold on to the past and coming to God will be a difficult task. So many unpleasant things could have taken place in an individual's past. Our past can be a vicious cycle from one generation to another. Some of the things which can travel through generations are:

- Child Abuse
- Spouse Abuse
- Alcohol Abuse (drunkenness)
- Whore Mongering, Adultery (sedition)
- Murder
- Lying

When we come to Christ, we are leaving a very dark past. Some situations have left lasting emotional marks and scars. Some of us have cheated, stolen, and fornicated against the very people whom we say we love. Second Corinthian 4:6 says, "For God, who commanded the light to shine out of darkness, hath shined in our hearts, to give the light of the knowledge of the glory of God in the face of Jesus Christ" (KJV).

Romans 2:3 says, "For we must all appear before the judgment seat of Christ; that everyone may receive the things done in his body, according to that he hath done, whether it be good or bad" (KJV).

Our past must be dealt with by taking an honest look at ourselves. Introspection is hard work when you really have to look at you regarding the things you have done. In order for God to lead souls through the door of salvation, one must be willing to let the old pass away. The past is a destroyer, a deceiver, and is not an indicator of what God is ready to do in your life. The enemy wants to keep you in debt to your past. In the past, old things are the sins committed against God. These were sins that had the mouth of Hell surrounding our everlasting life. Some things were brought over in Holiness with us after receiving Salvation. It was test and trails that surfaced them back up to us (Guthery, p 25).

Let me say test and trails meet you where you are at. They better you, but temptation led you from where you are going and deceive you (Guthery, p 26). Temptation draws you away of your own lust and entice you. Test and trials produce in you, and patience, experiences, and hope make you not be ashamed (Study Reading: James chapter 1). Test make you and temptations break you. When your past is not dead, lust will try to lead you away from God. That is why we must be dead to our past transgressions and sins. We must not be double-minded about doing what is right. It is either right or wrong and black or white. But you may say it's complicated, I get that. It just might be, but you have to examine what is the truth about your situation. Letting the old man go, the past things, the dark, ugly, old, and past things can be hard but very much necessary; that is, if you want to grow.

We must stop using the phrase "I can't help it." I can't tell you how many times I have used that phrase to God. We sometimes justify or at least attempt to justify the reason why we can't live saved or the reason why we continue in sin. I call it the I-can't-help-it syndrome. During these times of our pity party, when we know we have just done wrong, we will use phrases like God knows my heart. But here in lies the problem. God really does know your heart, and, in some cases, He sees your heart is wicked. "The Bible says the heart is deceitful above all things, and desperately wicked; who can know it?" (Jeremiah 17:9).

We must trust our new life in God once we have "denied" ourselves. The past cannot harm the future in God. We must "remember God's Word and know that all things are of God who hath reconciled us to himself by Jesus Christ, and hath given to us the ministry of reconciliation" (2 Corinthians 4:18). "To wit, that God was in Christ reconciling the world unto himself, not imputing their trespass unto them and hath committed unto us the ministry of reconciliation" (v 19). "For he hath made him to be sin for us, who knew no sin; that we might be made the righteousness of God in him" (v 21, KJV).

LETTING GO OF THE PAST

> For he saith, "I have heard thee in a time accepted, and in the day of salvation have succored thee; behold, now is the acceptable time behold, now is the day of salvation. Giving no offense in anything, that the ministry be not blamed." (2 Corinthians 6:1–2) (Study Reading 1 Corinthians 6:1–18)

It is time to "come out from among them and be ye separated, saith the Lord, and touch not the unclean thing and I will receive you" (2 Corinthians 6:17). Recognize the past sins, acknowledge that the sins were committed against God, and let go. Repent and turn around. "Have mercy upon me oh God, according to thy loving kindness according to thy tender mercies, blot out my transgressions" (Psalm 51).

We must be sorry for how we have treated God. The New Age Gospel teaches that there is no need to be sorry for your sins anymore because it teaches that God knows your heart because we are human. Sins are not really completely the focus of our problems—just your deliverance, faith, and healing—oh yes, and prosperity. This philosophy will have you focus on only on what God can do for you rather than what you need to do for God.

David declared, "Wash me through from my iniquity and cleanse me from my sin. We must deal with the sin issue. Church has come to the place of the haves and have nots? We have become comfortable, too mundane, where is faith, the faith that was once delivered to the saints. Where are the praying mothers who like Rachel in the book of Jeremiah, who refuse to be comforted as they prayed for their sons and daughters?"

Hebrews 11:23 says, "By faith Moses when he was born, was hid three months of his parents because they seen he was a proper child." Moses was hidden because he had an assignment by God. Moses's assignment was to be a deliverer of an entire nation. If you examine his life, it started off pretty rocky and got better, and then he ended losing everything. God has a way of showing us our end from our beginning (Ephesians 1) and then backing us all the way up and starting us over. Just like Moses, we all have assignments that we must complete. Your assignment may be to get out of that extramarital affair but to learn from it so that you can be a help to others. Your assignment could be the sin that you presently have in your life, your job, your troubled kids, your debt, or your sickness. But God wants you to know how the devil looks, smell, and work, so when you get out of this one, you will know the devil when you see him. If you are currently in a test, it is to prompt your faith in God. Hebrews 11:24 says, "By faith Moses, when he was come to years, refused to be called the son of Pharaoh's daughter." When you mature in God, you no longer want the stuff that the devil or others have given you to keep you in debt or bound to them. You can date a person and realize that you don't have to sell yourself by accepting gifts from someone knowing they are going to want something in return.

You can tell them to come get their lamp back and "these cloths you bought me and the jewelry, and here's your house keys back. And you can keep the car because I don't need that. I'm going to Deny myself, so I can get what God has for me. I'm going to shake the I-can't-help-it and realize that faith is not about stuff and things. Faith is the power I got in the spirit to believe!"

In the book of Philippians 3:7–11, Paul tells us:

> But what things were gain to him, those he counted loss for Christ. Yea doubtless, and I count all things loss for the excellency of the knowledge of Christ Jesus my Lord: for whom I have suffered the loss of all things, and do count them but dung, that I may win Christ, and be found in him, not having my own righteousness, which is of the law, but that which is through the faith of Christ, the righteousness which is of God by faith: that I may know him, and the power of his resurrection and the fellowship of his sufferings, being made conformable unto his death. If

by any means I might attain unto the resurrection of the dead. (KJV)

During my time of suffering, I realized that the stuff and things that I once possessed were nice, but anytime you put stuff in things before God, you have just made an idol. I believe in me learning how to Deny myself. I realized that God was not provision, stuff, and things, but He was my source—my everything—and my Alpha and Omega. He was also everything in between.

I realized that when I was at my worst of everything I lost, when I went to the gas station with only the $20 dollars that I had in my pocket and didn't know where or when I was going to have any money again, I learned how to pump gas, thanking and praising God for the little that I had. Before I had money, before I had three cars, and before I never stopped to thank God for the money to pay for gas, it was a given. What I realize was, as I denied myself, I was winning Christ. Like Paul, I began to count everything that I had as nothing, dung, because now through nature, through people, through the Holy Spirit, and through reading my Bible, I am winning Christ. I'm getting to know Him in a way money would not allow me to.

I'm beginning to know Christ, just know Him, in the fellowship of His suffering. If Christ had to suffer, why do we feel as though we shouldn't or won't have to suffer? I know our society and even our church teaches us to win, but what happens when you begin to lose and no one can't explain to you why? Well, I can tell you exactly what's happening to you. God wants you to deny yourself so that you can win Him.

We can grow and mature spiritually as we continue to trust Christ and learn more about him by drawing closer to him and obeying him. Our progress is changeable because it depends on our daily walk. At times in life, we mature more than at other times. But we are growing toward perfection if we work toward it. These good works do not perfect us. Rather, as God perfects us, we do good works for him. We are grounded by our faith in Christ and what he has done, not what we can do for him. We cannot perfect ourselves.

Only God can work in and through us "until the day of Jesus Christ" (Philippians 1:6).

LEAVING SOME THINGS BEHIND

I think it's important to mention that in the same chapter of Philippians 3, Paul wrote:

> Though I might also have confidence in the flesh. If any other man thinks that he hath whereof he might trust in the flesh, I more. Circumcised the eighth day, of the stock of Israel, of the tribe of Benjamin, a Hebrew of the Hebrews; as touching the law, a Pharisee; concerning zeal, persecuting the church; touching the righteousness which is in the law, blameless.

At first glance at this, it seems that Paul is boasting about his achievements. But actually, he is doing the opposite. Showing the human achievements, no matter how impressive, it cannot earn a person salvation and eternal life with God. Paul had impressive credentials: upbringing, nationality, family background, inheritance, orthodoxy, activity, and morality (see 2 Corinthians 11; Galatians 1:13–24 for more details on his credentials). But his conversion to faith in Christ in Acts 9 wasn't based on his credentials but upon the grace of Christ "for by grace and we saved through faith" (Ephesians 2:8). Paul did not depend on his credentials to please God because even the most impressive credentials fall short of God's Holy standards. Credentials, accomplishments, or reputation cannot earn salvation. Are you depending on Christian parents, your church affiliation, or just being good to make you right with God? You must realize that salvation comes only through faith in Christ.

In this text, Paul's response was to a group of people called the Judaizers. These were Jewish people who attempted to mix elements of the Law of Moses with the grace of God given through Christ. They were trying to get Gentile believers to adopt various elements of the Jewish lifestyle in order to ensure their salvation. The Apostle Paul, however, consistently confronts these men and declares that you cannot add anything to what God through Christ has done for us. Christ paid it all on Calvary.

These Judaizers apparently claimed certain superiority over the Gentiles, probably even pointing out that Jesus Himself was a Jew. They attempted to go further by trying to cast Paul in a negative light to make themselves look better. Paul, however, is ready to pull out his resume and place it up against anything that these men had to offer. After laying out his resume above, it was doubtful that not any of the Judaizer could contend with his resume. Paul was explaining that God gave the Law of Moses and the law is good, but God gave us something far better than the law when He sent His Only begotten Son down to earth to die for the sins for the world. It's no longer about trying to make myself acceptable. It is now about being accepted through Christ. It's about being something that I could never achieve in my flesh. It is about righteousness obtained by faith and not by works but by His love and not the law, and by his fellowship and not by formality. It is righteousness obtained by relationship through faith and not by ritual, religion, or race.

Paul said, "It's no more law I want to learn. It's not more religion I want to practice. It's not more favor in the eyes of man that I desire. It's not more Atta boys I want to achieve on my job. But I want to know Him, Christ, and the power of his resurrection and the fellowship of his suffering becoming more and more like him (even) in his death." And nothing I desire compares to that! You can find yourself in loss of a lot of things—family friends and loved ones that were so dear, but it does not compare to losing Jesus and then finding Him in your frailty. Finding Christ or, should I say, Christ finds us right where we're at. You can be at the bottom of a bottle, but Christ can find you. You can be walking over "hell" on a spider web, but Christ can find you because before you ever thought to pursue after Him, he already perused after you, and while you were dead in sins and trespasses, Christ died for you.

In order to win Christ and truly know you have Him, you will have to recognize that there are some things you are going to have to leave behind, and there are some things that you are going to have to forget. Now this can be a very hard thing to do because you may have created ungodly soul ties or inner vows and bitter root judgments or through sin, doubt or unbelief, or a traumatic experience, and from un-forgiveness, bitterness, and resentment, you may have opened a portal for demonic influences in your life (Piscopo, p 153). But if you have done some introspection, looked at your associations with people, and moved your pride out of the way and repented, you are on your way to forgetting those things which are behind.

Paul wrote in Philippians 3:12–14:

> Not as though I had already attained, either were already perfect: but I follow after, if that I may apprehend that for which also I am apprehended of Christ Jesus. Brethren, I count not myself to have apprehended: but this one thing I do, forgetting those things which are behind, and reaching forth unto those things which are before I press toward the mark for the prize of the high calling of God in Christ Jesus.

Paul admits that the Christian faith is a journey, and he hasn't arrived yet. Many of us are on that journey called life, yet it's more than life journey that we are on. God is placing us on assignment, and the first assignment is dealing with you. You haven't arrived until you get there, but you have to get there first. "Like newborn babes, desire the sincere milk of the word that ye may grow" (1 Peter 2:2).

Paul said, "This one thing I do: Forgetting those things which are behind me and reaching straining, toward those things that are ahead of me, I press toward the goal to win the prize in Christ Jesus."

What prize? It is to live and die as a reflection of the character of Christ so that you may obtain the resurrection unto eternal life of which Jesus was the first fruits—the example for us to follow. If you don't seek to obtain that, then nothing else really matters.

> Jesus says, if any man is to come after me let him deny himself and take us his cross and follow me.

> For whosoever will save his life shall lose it: and whosoever will lose his life for my sake shall find it. For what is a man profit, if he shall gain the whole world, and lose his own soul? Or what shall a man give in exchange for his soul. For the Son of man shall come in the glory of his Father with his angels; and then he shall reward every man according to his works. (Matthew 16:24–27)

Jesus Christ has been given the authority to judge all the earth (Philippians 2:9–11). Although his judgment is already working in our lives, there is a future final judgment when Christ returns (25:21–46), and everyone's life will be reviewed and evaluated. This will not be confined to nonbelievers. Christians too will face a judgment. Their eternal destiny is secure, but Jesus will look at how they handled gifts, callings, opportunities, and responsibilities in order to determine their heavenly rewards. At the time of judgment, God will deliver the righteous and condemn the wicked. We should not judge others' salvation; that is God's work.

Paul stated that in order to press on to the prize, we are going to have to be willing to leave some things behind. To press means:

- To take action or press or pull.
- To move by means of pressure.
- To act upon through steady pushing or thrusting force vented in content.
- And to follow through, to take authority over.

Paul is saying that I have to push through and leave some things in the process. I'm going to leave those things that I thought mattered most to me. Those things that I once took pride in. Those things that I once defended and defined my life. Those things that others brag about: new position, new car, bigger salary, and perfect marriage. Paul said I now count those things, but dung, I'm leaving those things behind so that I can press and take authority over my life, so I can take action, move forward, be stable enough to move forward, and get on with my life.

If we intend on obtaining God's blessing, his provision, and God's favor in this new season in our lives, it just might take us leaving some things behind. If we are not careful, we can become entangled and bog down with everything that has happened to us over the course of the last few years, and our entire lives will fail to move forward in God. This happens to individuals and to churches who have not decided to Deny themselves and to follow God. If we continue to refuse to let go, then all we have is another year of what we just had. If you always do what you have always done, you will always be where you have always been.

Paul said I'm leaving those things I once treasured. Leaving the good old days. He had once been proud of his religion, but then he found something better in Jesus. Until we release the past, we can never embrace the future. I know it hurts. I know you suffer from depression, loneliness, rejection, and abandonment. But you are going to have to dig up the bones, deal with your situation, and leave those things behind. Jesus will turn your scars into stars. You must not dwell on where you have been but look and understand where God is taking you.

Paul said he was going to leave behind tradition. He had been brought up in the Jewish religion and tradition. As an adult, he sought to rise to an elevated position among his peers. But what Paul tells us is that he never found the atonement of others until he died to self. He said, "I am crucified with Christ and I no longer live, but Christ lives in me. The life that I live in the body, I Live by faith in the son of God, who loved me and gave himself for me" (Galatians 2:20).

If we are not careful, we will simply fall in a rut and run in religious and emotional circles that lead us back to where we started. Paul was willing to leave behind everything he thought he knew about being religious so that he could enter into relationship with Jesus Christ. Leaving tradition means that we are willing to honor our past without forsaking our future.

Paul was willing to leave his mistakes. Paul testifies in a couple places in the Scripture that he had been guilty of persecuting the church (Acts 8:3). Paul listed this as one of the things that he was willing to leave behind. If we allow Satan to keep us in debt to him by being a stronghold in our lives because we can't or refuse because of fear to let go of somebody or something, then Satan will tie us up in our mistakes to our shame, fear, and condemnation.

Finally Paul was willing to leave behind the hatred against any who had wronged him. Now this is hard to do, but you must consider yourself that there are times when you have hurt people maybe on purpose or by chance, but chances are, people have hurt you as well. You must be willing to let go and let God, and forgive your brother or sister of their trespasses, and God delivers you from your trespasses and sins. Notice it says trespasses. There were some places in your life that you were not supposed to take your body to or join it with whomever because you were trespassing (Matthew 6:9–14). Paul concerning the law was blameless. Contrary to those challenging Paul's credentials to preach the Gospel, Paul declares that he had upheld the highest standard of the law and still decided that God was doing something far better in Christ that his schooling or religion could ever do. He could have held anger and malice and discontent in his heart toward those who tried to elevate themselves by putting him down. But Paul said, "I'm leaving those things behind."

Paul had reason to feel sorrow about the past. He held the coats of those who stoned Stephen, the first Christian martyr (Acts 7:57–58, Paul was called Saul here). We have all done things for which we are ashamed, and we all live in the tension of what we have been and what we want to be. Because of our hope in Christ, we can let go of the past guilt and look forward to what he will help us become. Don't dwell on the past. I'm telling you, it can keep your life tied up for years. Instead, grow in the knowledge of God concentrating on your relationship with him now. Realize you are forgiven, and then move on to a life of faith and obedience. Look forward to a fuller and more meaningful life because of your hope in Christ.

CHAPTER 9

Take Up Your Cross To Be a Prisoner of the Lord…(Matthew 16:24)

Whoever does not bear his own cross and come after me cannot be my disciple.

—Luke 14:27

What is a Cross? Webster defines a cross as a mark, an object, or figure by two short intersecting lines or pieces. If you really think about it a cross, it is just a piece of mental or wood or stick. Or even if you use your fingers to make a cross, it's just two lines that intersect into one. What is the meaning of the Cross? Simply put, the (real) meaning of a cross means death. From the BC 6th century until the 4th century AD, the cross was an instrument of execution that resulted in death by the most torturous and painful of ways. In crucifixion, a person was either tied or nailed to a wooden cross and left to hang until dead. Death would be slow and excruciating painful; in fact, the word excruciating literally means "out of crucifying." However, because of Christ's death on the cross, the meaning of the cross today is completely different. Before Christ's death on the cross, many had died such a cruel death. But the cross nowadays is a symbol of hope and salvation. How could something so bloody be used to bring salvation to those who believe in faith?

It's because the Cross reveals to us the character of God. The cross of Jesus Christ is the central theme to the Christian faith. The Cross shows God's love for us (sinners), and His perfect justice meets at the cross. If we want to grow in our love for God (which is the greatest commandment), then we must grow to understand and appreciate the cross. If we want to grow in godliness, we must grow in understanding the significance of the cross, which confronts the most prevalent and insidious of all sins namely pride.

The Cross is the place where all our wounds of sin are healed. If you suffer from mental or emotional or even physical problems, guilt, anxiety, depression, anger, fear, bitterness, rejection, abandonment, or whatever your problem is, it is healed at the Cross of Jesus Christ. If you have lost a loved one or if you're facing impossible situations in your life or if you are suffering through a tragedy, there is comfort in the Cross of Jesus Christ. Isaiah 53:5 says, "But He was wounded for our transgressions, He was crushed for our iniquities, and the chastening for our wellbeing fell upon Him, and with His scourging (stripes) we are healed" (KJV).

If you are unable to deny yourself, you will never be able to see and understand the true call that God has on your life. I'm not necessarily talking about a call into ministry, but I'm referring to the Scripture Matthew 16:24, "if any man is to come after me, let him deny himself and take up his cross and follow me."

You see, you may never die for your love of your friends or the love of your family or the love of your job, but if you are going to learn or understand or come after God to gain a deeper understanding of who he is, then you're going have to deny yourself in order for you to truly come in the presence of God. Understand this: I'm not talking about you to come as you are into salvation. God accepts you just as you are. The truth is, while you were in sins and trespasses, Christ died for you.

So while you were on the dance-room floor down at Floods or Nicki's or anywhere else, Christ died for you. He already paid the price for you to have enteral life. But we have to catch up to what Christ already has done. He already paid for your peace of mind. He already paid for your joy, and Christ already paid for your healing and your salvation. It was all done on the Cross. You just have to learn to walk in what Christ has already paid for. If someone told you they paid for you a house when you've been living on the street, you would get mad if you asked them the question, "How long have I had this house, and no one told me about it?" And the answer you received back was, "You had this house for years. Either you didn't know it or you didn't believe it, but it was always yours." Well, that's how salvation is. Christ died that you may live.

Here's the problem: only prisoners carry crosses while free men do not carry a cross. Those who love themselves will never take up their cross. The cross means a sentence to death. The cross means you got to stop doing what you want to do. The cross means that you got to be willing to lay your life down for others. The cross does not feel good. The cross certainly doesn't look good, and for those who live by how they feel, you will find the cross unbearable. The cross is intended to bring your life to an end so that you can pass through death and come on to Resurrection Ground. Romans 8:1 states, "Therefore, there is now no condemnation for those who are in Christ Jesus. Verse 2, because through Christ Jesus the law of the Spirit who gives life has set you free from the law of sin and death" (King James Version).

Since most Christians believe their spiritual life is at its highest, whenever they "feel" spiritual, they deem it to be at its lowest whenever they "feel" unspiritual. As long as praise and prayer is flowing, then they must be doing the right thing. As long as they are getting revelation and church and attending Bible classes and they can see that their works are paying off for them, then they feel that they are on the right track. But if ever they feel alone or unsure, uneasy or dreary in their walk, they (incorrectly) believe that they have lost something of their former status as a believer.

We must come to understand that our spiritual life has very little to do with how we feel. Spiritual life has everything to do with our position in the Lord. You can feel bad or sick or tired. That doesn't mean that you are not powerful or mighty in God or that you lost your spiritual life. A lot of Christians feel that their spiritual life is at its highest when they feel spiritual and believe that it's at its lowest when they feel unspiritual. This is because they believe that the Lord only wants positive, bright, delicious, and happy feelings of them. The reality is that they have mistaken a life of feeling for a life of Faith. Romans 10:17 tells us to "walk by faith and not by sight."

A PRISONER OF THE LORD

The truth is that when we are young, we may dress ourselves and go about as we wish. But true spiritual growth is less of me and more of Him. The true evidence of growth is not how we feel about ourselves or what other people judge us to be. Our spiritual walk is not the sum of all our wonderful experiences and feelings. True growth is the decreasing of SELF and the increasing of CHRIST. True spiritual power is based in weakness, not strength. True "spiritual life" is based on death: Death to self and death to the things of this world. Galatians 2:20 states, "it is no longer I but Christ that lives through me." So when we are older in the Lord, we may no longer lead ourselves, but we stretch forth our hands and allow another to dress and lead us where we would not chose to go, yet it is as necessary as it is inevitable.

Young Christians, in their ability to dress themselves, want to do something because they are zealous. They want to change the world; they say it, and they do it. Young people are full of plans. Proverbs 19:21 says, "There are many plans in a man's heart but the counsel (purpose) of the Lord it will stand."

Jeremiah 29 says, "I know the thoughts I have towards you plans of peace and to give you and excepted end."

God has plans for us, and He is ready to put us on assignment. But the real question is not what I say, do, or where I go. The real question is, do I glorify God in what I say, where I go, or in what I do? Whenever "I" do something, I consider it spiritual and good. It is, nevertheless, "me" who does it. Often, we do what glorifies us. The Lord and his need are seldom considered. But when we ask what glorifies the Lord, we see that the Lord is glorified when He is able to dress us and lead us where He wants us to go with no interference from ourselves.

Spiritual maturity is not being able to do more or less. It's being able to do nothing of myself. God is more glorified in my "death" than in my "life." It is most difficult for people to see this. They have been told that God "hired" them to put them to work for His kingdom. If they don't report or "work" every week, then they are told God's kingdom suffer loss. Instead of the Lord's easy yoke and light burden, religion gives them a difficult yoke and heavy burden.

When you are young, you may dress yourself, but after some time, the Lord begins to touch those things that matter, and we find it difficult to live, move, or do anything of our own accord. Self begins to be replaced with Christ, and someone else begins to dress us up and take us to places where we would not wish to go. The Lord's prisoners are really at liberty even though they are bound. Ephesians 3:1:

1. For this reason, I, Paul, the prisoner of Christ Jesus for the sake of the Gentiles.
2. Surely you have heard about the administration of God's grace that was given to me for you.
3. That is, the mystery made known to me by revelation, as I have already written briefly.
4. In reading, this then, you will be able to understand my insight into the mystery of Christ,
5. Which was not made known to people in other generations as it has now been revealed by the Spirit to God's holy apostle and prophets.
6. This mystery is that through the gospel the gentiles are heirs together with Israel, members together of one body, and heirs together in the promise in Christ Jesus.
7. I became a servant of this gospel by the gift of God's grace given me through the working of his power.
8. Although I am less than the least of all the Lord's people, this grace was given me: to preach to the Gentiles the boundless riches of Christ,
9. And to make plan to everyone the administration of this mystery, which for ages past was kept hidden in God, who created all things.

10. His intent was that now, through the church, the manifold wisdom of God should be made known to the rulers and authorities in the heavenly realms,
11. According to his eternal purpose that he accomplished in Christ Jesus or Lord.
12. In Him and through faith in Him we may approach God with freedom and confidence.
13. I ask you, therefore, not to be discouraged because of my sufferings for you, which are your glory.

Paul is saying to us that we have a right to Praise and Worship God too. When you are a prisoner of the Lord, you cannot go where you want to go or do what you want to do. 1st Peter 2:9 says, "For ye are a chosen generation a royal priest-hood a holy nation a peculiar people, that you should shew forth the praises on him who brought you out of darkness into His marvelous light." The difference between the young saints and old saints or babies and mature saints is the young are independent and free. If the way is blocked, they work at once to break through the blockage. They never consider that perhaps the way is blocked because they are still dressing and leading themselves. But the older saints that know the Lord are not independent and free. They are restricted like a prisoner because someone else decides if they will or will not go, what they will or will not say, and what they will or will not do.

There is a liberty that is really not a liberty at all. It is a kind of disguised bondage. Many will proclaim themselves to be "free" when it should be clear that true freedom is not the ability to do as I please or to be free from doing as I please for when I do as I please, when I follow my own will and my own way, it just leads to more bondage.

If we look at things from another point of view, there is a bondage that is really not bondage at all. It is a kind of disguised liberty. The prisoners of the Lord know something of this "disguised liberty." By stretching forth their arms to be dressed and led about by another, they seem to be throwing away their rights. How strange we think that the Lord often puts His greatest ambassadors in Chains—literally and figuratively. But the prisoners of the lord have more liberty in their "bondage" than most people have in their "liberty."

What does it mean to be a prisoner of the Lord? It means that we are not our own. We have been bought with a price, and we do not belong to this world. We don't belong to this earth. We don't even belong to the Church. We are the Lord's Peculiar possession. As the prisoner of the Lord, we give up our rights. We give up our independent ways and submit ourselves to His will and His kingdom in all things.

Now when we first come to the Lord, we truly think we are giving Him all of us, but we cannot fully appreciate just how powerful SELF is. It cannot be dealt with in a once or for all manner. It requires many seasons of God's dealings for us to see the truth about the Lord and the truth about ourselves. That is why there is more hope for someone who is ready to give up and quit than there is for someone who keeps promising to do better tomorrow. Only after we have tried and failed one hundred, one million, or one thousand times will we at last be able to say, "Lord, I finally understand now that I can originate nothing on my own self because whenever I do, I'm met with nothing but defeat. So I'm finished. I'm done." God shared with me after all of the losses I shared with you in Chapter 1 that all of my VICTORIES are in Him and Him alone. None and not one are in me anymore because it is not my will, but God's will shall be done in my life. It is only after God has uncovered or exposed you and made us to feel uncomfortable that God really and truly get the Glory out of our lives.

These words are not uttered easily. Anyone can mouth these words and give their mental reasoning to them, but their behavior all too often contradicts their confession. So the Lord must labor long and hard to work into us, a heart attitude, and not just a lip service. Many Christians wonder why their circumstances are so difficult. They wonder why things never seem to go their way or come together for them. They wonder why everything seems to rise up and challenge them. The primary reason for this is that the Lord intends to reduce you to Himself and make you His prisoner.

As prisoner of the Lord, we have no control over our environment, our going out, or our coming in. The truth is that control is just a mere illusion. "The winds blow where He wishes it to go and you cannot tell where He is coming from and where He is going" (John 3:8). So often, we think that we have God, the Bible, the Church, and our Christian life figured out. We have answers for every single question. What happens when you don't understand what God is doing in your life? What happens when you cannot figure out what your next move or step is going to be?

You are at a place where if Jesus doesn't do this thing in your life for you, then it won't be done. Resources gone, money gone, no job, friends, gone, and your family can't help. We normally have the solution to every problem. But suddenly, the winds shift, and we realize we don't know anything. Neither do we have it all together. We learn that we do not move the wind, but the wind moves us. This is God's way of decreasing us and increasing Him in us. We learn from experience that "apart from God, I'm nothing without Him and I can do nothing apart from Him" (John 15:5).

To be a prisoner of the Lord means that we accept the sentence of death and are resigned to our fate. We are not the Lord's prisoner if we are still protesting our innocence. If we do not agree with the Lord that the SELF is worthy of death, then we unnecessarily "delay the inevitable." Remember this because I will address the spirit of delay in the next few chapters.

We delay the inevitable when we refuse to die to self and to allow Christ to live in and through us. If we must take up the Cross and be crucified, it is better to submit ourselves to it as Christ did, giving up our spirit into the Father's hands, and bowing our head in peace. So we must drink for the CUP that the Father gave us. If we struggle and protest like the two thieves, then we only prolong our agony, and the soldiers must come and break our legs. Either way, the Cross means death. The sooner we surrender to it, the sooner we find resurrection. We must die to self and die out to the way we have done things in the past.

What is a cross? It is an instrument of death, and yet in still, you see people wearing a cross around their necks every day. Do they really die daily? Remember, only prisoners carry crosses; free men don't. Those who love themselves will never take up their cross. The cross means a sentence to death. It does not feel good, and for those who live by how they feel, they will find the Cross uncomfortable and unbearable. The cross is intended to bring your life to an end so that you can pass through death and come on to Resurrection Ground.

You see, for me, I realized in my boss's office right before I was to be let go that God was trying to tell me something. When I made the statement that I had been here in this place in my life before, I was saying that I had been in a place where I was vulnerable to God, and most of the times when we are in a place of vulnerability, we don't want to give up control of us. God was trying to stop me from doing me. He wanted me to start doing things His way because He knew the plans that He had for me, and I was wasting time. Jeremiah 29:11 says, "I know the plans I have for you, declares the Lord, 'plans to prosper you and not harm you, plan to give you hope and a future.'" I'm talking about a total difference.

I had been running from my future with God for years, trying to climb the cooperate ladder, trying to be in charge, and trying to be the man that everyone else wanted me to be. But here I was, living a lie in most of the times in my life, hurting good people by trying to be something that I was not, and wishing to be someone who I really wasn't. You do realize that wherever purpose is not known, abuse is inevitable. I spent years just like Samson abusing my purpose and looking for love in all the wrong places to find that I had real love all the time when I found Jesus. When you truly take an honest look at all the people you hurt when you don't know who you are, all I can say is, "Lord, forgive me," but then hurting people is one thing because people have choices in the matter as well, but what about the damages and the hurt that you bring upon yourself when you don't understand your purpose in God?

The cross is bloody. The cross hurts. It tortures. It's suffering. But in order to achieve greatness in God, you, like an athlete, must put this body and mind and spirit through rigorous training. That's why we must deny ourselves because we can never go through the training that is needed for us to endure until we deny ourselves so that it's no longer about us but about God's Glory being seen in us. Jesus said, "If any man is to come after me, let him deny himself." The Apostle Paul said in 1 Corinthians 9:27, "I beat my body and bring it into submission, for fear that by any means that after I have preached to others that I myself become a cast away."

Matthew 16:24 says, "If any man is to come after me let him deny himself and take up his cross and follow me." This may be the most important description of what it means to be a follower of Jesus in the entire Gospel. But as discussed before, most of us have no idea what it really means. It means self-denial. It means denying ourselves instead of fulfilling ourselves. It means stop doing what you want to do.

No, it does seem like Jesus did not ask a fair question for us to deny ourselves. But it is a glorious thing to be a prisoner of the Lord for in our bonds, we find liberty. In our weakness, we find strength. In our poverty, we find prosperity. By losing everything, we find everything. By giving up all things, we inherit all things. By accepting the sentence of death, we find the life of the Lord. Let us stretch forth our hands and allow Him to dress us and lead us where He wishes us to go in the way we would not choose for ourselves.

Finally the cross means death. You have to die to self every day. Paul stated in 1 Corinthians 15:31, "I protest by your rejoicing which I have in Christ Jesus our Lord, I die daily." Let us not think that we can continue in sin after we are saved by allowing your circumstances to help you become more like Christ, especially the circumstances you don't like or feel like you want to deal with a certain problem. Anytime you feel the pain of rejection, abandonment, suffering, physical challenge, injustice, failure, trials, and tribulations is an opportunity to die to self, pride, and sin. You have to keep dying to self daily, and you will come alive in ways you never could imagine.

Chapter 10

The Cross of Loss

For you have died and your life is hidden with Christ in God.

—Colossians 3:3

In the early chapters, I shared with you regarding my loss, but I remember sitting in my living room one day, and I was praying, and I asked God to show me His Glory. The answer that I received from God was that, "I am going to show you my Glory, but it's not going to be the way you expected it to be." You see, I thought that I was going to experience God's Glory like Moses did when the Lord placed him in the cleft of the rock in Exodus 33:22, "...and when my glory passes by, I will put you in the cleft of the rock and cover you with my hand until I pass by." Moses was able to see God hinder parts Himself. However, my experience was not that I had just lost my grandmother early that year, my son, my mother was in a comma, and my job. I'm saved but not delivered from my own issues, and now my wife is in the hospital, and she is not looking well at all. I just wanted to see God's Glory!

I wanted to see what He had shown me so many times before, and that's Him showing up in my situation and showing out and what did God mean anyway by saying that His Glory was not going to be what I expected. As the days went by, I realized that I had no money coming in, and every bill was due, and there was no money to pay them.

The last time I was employed, I had a 401K and a ROLF IRA to bounce back on. I was able to stay off of work for almost two years taking care of my wife without batting an eye. But now I'm starting to lose things like people and jobs. Now I couldn't pay my car notes for three cars, and they are calling me to come get the cars. My unemployment is tied up, and I have no income. Thank God for a few family and friends that gave me money to stop the bleeding. I applied for general assistance and was only able to get help that added up to $196 every month.

What was God doing to me? Didn't he care? Didn't He see my needs? I got angry with God, but I tried not to doubt because I didn't want to block my blessing. I got angrier at God because here I have been in church all my life, and when I need Him the most, I can't find Him or hear from Him. In my mind, I had to remember the wonderful, miraculous things He had done for me and my family in the past. Then the unthinkable happened. The hospital calls and they tell me that my wife had coded, and she is in the ICU. I woke up on a Sunday morning to hear this all on my voice mail.

I called the hospital to find out what floor and room she was in. I rushed to the hospital to see her in the ICU, and she looks like everything is fine. She looked at me in my eyes and told me, "Sax, I feel like I'm dying. I say the only thing that I know to say which is God's Word. Helena, 'to be absent from the body is to be present with the Lord.'" She then closes her eyes and dies right before my face. This couldn't be God's Glory. This couldn't be God's will for my life. We, church folk those that know God, were more than conquerors. I know how to pray. I have watched and have seen miracles performed in my presence. I have laid hands on the sick and watch them recover.

Why didn't I tell her to get up? Why didn't I tell her that you are healed in Jesus's name and rebuke death? She had lived nine years longer than the doctors expected when they gave her date on June 4, 2005, to die. Where is everyone else at? Why am I here all by myself? Why do I feel left alone and abandoned?

I have no job. I have no wife. I have no money. I'm losing everything—my cars, my condo, my stuff, and my mind! Why won't anyone help me? Look at all the people I have helped through the years. Where are they at now? Traitors, liars—all of them! Where are they all at now? But in reality, I had been lying to myself. How many times do you love other people properly without loving yourself adequately?

The church teaches us to win. They don't prepare people to lose. The church and the world mostly judge you by what you have or what you have obtained. They measure God in your life with a measuring stick by seeing what you possess. But what happens when you find yourself losing everything? Is it or could it be the "Devil"? It couldn't be God causing you to lose because God doesn't lose. He's not a loser. It must be because of sin in your life. Or it must be because you did something wrong.

At that time, for me, it could have been because of sin and everything else that I had did wrong in my life. I had a master's degree but could not get a job. I know a lot of people in high places, but no one could or would help me. What happens when you had been indoctrinated to WIN, WIN, WIN, but all you keep doing is LOSE, LOSE, LOSING MORE? I'm Job, and I'm hurting. I'm in my gethsemane, and I'm being crushed and bruised and forced to deal with myself and deal with my shortcoming and deal with my lies and deal with my false gods—the things that I put in front of the true and Living God.

Where are my friends now? Where are those that say they love me? Where is the family that I've given to for years? Bitterness and resentment and hatred and anger set in, and blame and shame and fear and rejection and abandonment and envy set in when you suffer from loss.

Losing a spouse to me was hard but even harder was the secondary losses I was experiencing, and I didn't even know it. To me, I felt as though I was totally exposed, and because the church doesn't teach you how to lose, I felt as though I lost God in the process too.

I soon realize that I was handicapped. There is a handicapped person in your future as well: you! Handicapped persons are dealing in the present moment with what you and I will have to deal with later. Sooner or later, each of us will have to deal with one or several major losses in our life and/or health. Then we will travel down the same path that the handicapped person currently walks. Then we will know their pain, frustration, and sufferings. Perhaps if we could learn from them now whatever our age, we would be better prepared for our own future (Wright, p 17)

Handicapped persons teach us that life is more than a body. They demonstrate the truth of all of the great religions that the things that make us truly human and truly divine are not the physical qualities. They are qualities of the Spirit. St. Paul listed a few of these qualities: love, joy, peace, patience, kindness, goodness, faithfulness, gentleness, and self-control (Galatians 5:22). Jesus listed a few more: meekness, peacemaking, purity of heart, mercy, hunger for righteousness, and suffering in a right cause (Matthew 5:3–10). Neither of them mentions physical beauty or even physical health. The qualities that save us do not include the shape of our bodies (Wright, p 17).

Handicapped persons also can teach us how to suffer and how to rise above bodily limitations. Sometimes, pain cannot be fixed nor can all limitations be conquered. Most of us will have to deal with pain and limitations—at first in minor ways and later in major ways. We will learn new meaning for the word "courage." Either we will rise above our limitations and learn to live with them or we shall sink to new lows of despair, bitterness, and helplessness. The choice depends largely of the strength of our courage.

In a sense, then a handicap or a loss of health can become a gift. It never starts out that way. Initially, it is a horrible loss. If through the loss, however, we can learn to nurture our spiritual qualities and learn the art of suffering well, then we will have transformed our loss into gain. We will have grown in and through our loss. We will have risen above our loss precisely by not letting it defeat us but by letting it propel us forward into a more advanced stage of human existence. Admittedly, not everyone makes such a major leap forward. Neither has some human beings made it past Sunday school theology, yet the loss of health in later life, as horrible as it seems, can be the opportunity for growing toward an ever greater level of spiritual maturity (Wright, p 18)

Whenever a loss occurs, it is important to see it in the context of your life experience, so you understand the full impact of what has happened. Identifying all of the accompanying losses as well as the impact of this loss on your thinking toward future events is important. Remember that past losses have an effect on current losses and attachments, and all of these factors affect your fear of future loss and your ability to make future attachments (Wright, p 20).

It is vital that you identify every loss in your life for what it is—a loss—and then grieve for it just as you would if someone died (Wright, p 21). Most people only identify a loss when a person dies, but there are many losses that occur in our lives: loss of a job, divorce, a relationship that ends, loss of a pet, and even loss of a friend who has moved away. When you don't grieve properly over those losses, unresolved reactions and feelings lead to a higher level of discomfort, and these unresolved issues continue to prevent us from living life to the fullest (Wright, p 21).

Every lesser loss that is experienced compounds the overall feeling of loss a person experiences. And each loss needs a grief reaction. Each one needs to be mourned. The meaning and extent of each loss varies for each person, depending on the investment that was made; thus, the amount of grieving required varies.

When a loss is permanent, it brings with it the sense that something has really ended. It is true that we might try to resist or avoid the reality, but when something is final, we do have to make a new life without its existence (Wright, p 24).

We must realize that in some instances, you may be involved in something, and you're trying to find your way out. God sometimes takes you through stages to bring you out of what you're in. There had been situations where we have gotten our own self in. Some of these situations will and could have people view your character as a monster. It's a lot of things I've been through, and it just was not me even though I was doing things that were wrong and against God. It wasn't me or the real person that I am. I did not realize any of this until I started losing things and people in my life. People are a crutch sometimes for you not to view what you are in your life to you. When you're not walking in the purpose of God in your life, abuse is inevitable. When you don't know what your purpose is, you're going to abuse yourself and others because you don't know where you're going, and you can't see or understand what God's will is for your life until you Deny yourself and take up your "loss" which happens to be your "cross" and follow Him.

Every loss is important. It is part of life and cannot be avoided. Losses are necessary. You grow by losing and then accepting the loss. Change occurs through loss. Growth occurs through loss. Life takes on a deeper meaning because of losses. The better you handle them, the healthier you will be and the more you will grow. No one said that loss was fair, but it is part of life. Loss can strengthen our faith. It enables us to trust more in God and His resources than in ourselves. God said to me, "I'm not just resources. I am the SOURCE." With every loss, we are reminded of the fact that we are not in control, and we are not self-sufficient. Every loss allows us to rest in the grace of God. Loss enables us to change our perspective and allows our hope and anticipation of the life to come to grow (1 Corinthians 4:19–20), "but I will come to you shortly, if the Lord will, and will know, not in speech of them which are puffed up, but the power. For the Kingdom of God is not in word but in Power." "What will ye? Shall I come unto you with a rod, or in love, and in the spirit of meekness?" (Wright, pg.36) (King James Version). Paul was directed by God to proclaim the message to us that we can rejoice or exult in our tribulations or sufferings.

Loss produces maturity. There are character qualities such as patience, endurance, humility, longsuffering, gratitude, and self-control that can develop through our losses.

> Moreover (let us also be full of joy now) let us exult and triumph in our troubles and rejoices in our suffering, knowing that pressure and affliction and hardship produce patient and answering endurance. And endurance (fortitude) develops maturity of character (approved faith and tried

integrity). And character (of this sort) produces (the habit of) joyful and confident hope of eternal salvation. (Romans 5:3–4)

We live in a world that demands immediate satisfaction. Losses teach us the lesson that it doesn't always work that way. We cannot have what we want when we want it no matter what.

When you experience a loss, like Paul, your beliefs can change. Paul discovered the purpose of loss. In 2 Corinthians 12:1–10, he talked about his thorn in the flesh. He wanted it to leave, and it wouldn't. But he learned that there was a purpose for this "thorn." God's power would be more evident in his life because of its presence. Second Corinthians 12:1–10:

1. I must go on boasting, although there is nothing to be gained. I will go to visions and revelations form the Lord.
2. I know a man in Christ who fourteen years ago caught up to the third heaven. Whether it was in the body or out of the body I do not know—God knows.
3. And I know that this man—whether in the body or apart from the body I do not know, but God knows.
4. Was caught up to paradise and heard inexpressible things, things that no one is permitted to tell.
5. I will boast about a man like that, but I will not boast about myself, except about my <u>weakness.</u>
6. Even if I should choose to boast, I would not be a fool, because I would be speaking the truth. But I refrain, so no one will think more of me than is warranted by what I do or say.
7. Or because of these surpassingly great revelations. Therefore, in order to keep me from becoming conceited, I was given a thorn in my flesh, a messenger or Satan, to torment me.
8. Three times I pleaded with the Lord to take it away from me.

9. But he said to me, "My grace is sufficient for you, for my power is made perfect in weakness." Therefore, I will boast all the more gladly about my weakness, so that Christ's power may rest on me.
10. That is why, in insults, in hardships, in persecutions, in difficulties. For when I am weak, then I am, strong (KJV).

So you see, even though I had lost everything that was near and dear to me and even though a lot of the loss was stuff and things, I realized as I was grieving I was also growing. I felt my strength come back and not the strength of being supported by having money in the bank or even having a job. I saw that no matter what state—physical, mental, emotional, or spiritual state of mind—I felt the love of Jesus in my heart. It was not about how much I had. I learned how to enjoy and to worship God out of my brokenness. It was out of the depths of my soul, body, mind, and spirit that I worshiped Him and thanked Him. It was not what I could do for Him to get His attention. It was what He was doing for me to get my attention. I was experiencing His Glory because what I went through, half of it would have drove someone else crazy, but it was my test for a testimony and hither to is where the Lord brought me.

So the way I define loss and why it is so painful is that loss is a broken attachment. It is devastating. It is so painful because in most cases, the thing that is loss is not replaceable because of the amount of value we have ascribed to it. It hurts so much because when something of value was taken away, you can never replace the original. When loss occurs, you feel violated. You feel a loss of control. The root of the offense of loss is unmet or (failed) expectations. The Scripture reference is Proverbs 18:19, "A brother offended is harder to win than a strong city" (KJV).

You move from the bondage of loss to freedom by embracing your emotions, identify (what you believe), and the reason why you feel the way that you do and change your mind (believe truth-specifically God's truth) about your situations.

I want to share with you that loss or trouble comes to everyone's life. No one is exempt—rich or poor and black or white. We will all experience loss or trouble. But in the real sense, trouble or loss, "through my eyes," are agents working for God.

1. Both Trouble and Loss when they come into your life, they demand your undivided attention.
2. Both Trouble and Loss comes to get you to take an honest look at yourself (introspection).
3. Both Trouble and Loss comes to rid you from certain people and associations.
4. Both Trouble and Loss can rid you from pride.
5. Both Trouble and Loss can humble you.
6. Both trouble and Loss can be well-springs of new discovery and things that you can learn about you when you are facing a trouble that only God can move or a loss that only God can heal.
7. Both trouble and Loss can rock you to your core and bring you to your knees, but while you're down there, you are going to have to give God some praise and let go and let God.

I want to be sure to mention that there is a difference between loss and grief. The definition of grief may vary, but it could be described as the valley of shadows, a deep remorse, anguish, and bitterness just to name a few emotions. It has been labeled everything from an intense mental anguish to acute sorrow to deep remorse. The difference between loss and grief is that the grieving process allows you to express these feelings of loss. Feelings are neither right nor wrong. They are just feelings. With each loss comes bitterness, emptiness, apathy, love, anger, guilt, sadness, fear, self-pity, and helplessness. The difference between loss and grief is that grief is the *response to the loss* (in class notes).

The purpose of grief is that it helps you to adjust to a new way of life. It helps you to move forward. The only way to get there is through the grieving process. The purpose of grief is to get you beyond the reaction to your loss such as anger, fear, and denial so that you can face your loss (Wright, p 41).

There are many problems in grieving and recovery. The key to remember is that through expression comes your healing. While I was grieving, I took everyone on my journey with me. I let people know how I was really feeling. When they asked me how I was, I didn't say I was okay. Just to give them an answer, I would tell them, "I don't know how I am today." And what bothers me more than anything was for someone to quote a Scripture and tell me it was going to be okay. It's easy for you to say everything is going to be okay when you are going back home to your normal life, but when you leave, I'm by myself, and nothing about my life is right or normal. Then you had the folks that would tell you I know how you feel. "No, you don't." What people don't realize is that when you have experienced loss, feelings are only valid to the person that is having them. And besides, it not just the loss that I'm grieving. In loss, you struggle with the fact that this person is no longer in my life because of death or divorce or broken relationship, then the fact remains as to who am I. Our value system was defined by what we did or didn't do with them. Now we have to learn how to live without them and that challenges who you are to your very core. Because sometimes, we are defined by our environment or by the people around us or by the powers that be. But when you suffer loss, if you can remember that no matter what you may have lost, you are God's child. And if you don't know or remember who you are, you can go to the Word of God, and it tells you who you are.

> You are a heir and joint heir with Jesus Christ. You are sons and daughters of God and it does not appear what you shall be but we know when He appears we shall be like Him for we shall see Him as He is. (1 John 3:2, KJV).

In defining recovery from loss and grief, you find that recovery is a process involving regaining your ability to function as you once did and resolving and integrating your loss into life. Recovery means to reinvest in life looking for relationships and new dreams. Recovery is where a newfound source of joy is possible. Remembering that the source of joy is in the Lord! God is the one who extends to you the invitation to reinvest in life.

What you discover in your recovery is that recovery is a choice. The change in your identity, relationships, new roles, and even abilities can be either positive or negative. This is where you have a choice (Wright, p 116).

When you experience loss, you will discover the extent of the comfort of God. Blessed be the God and Father of our Lord, Jesus Christ. The father of sympathy (pity and mercy) and the God (Who is the Source) of every comfort (consolation and encouragement) who comforts (consoles and encourages) us in every trouble (calamity and affliction) so that we may also be able to comfort (console and encourage) those who are in any kind of trouble or distress with the comfort (consolation and encouragement) with which we ourselves are comforted (consoled and encouraged) by God. For just as Christ's (own) sufferings fall to our lot (as they overflow upon His disciples, and we share and experience them) abundantly, so through Christ, comfort (consolation and encouragement) is also (shared and experienced) abundant by us.

But if we are troubled (afflicted and distressed), it is for your comfort (consolation and encouragement) and (for your) salvation. And if we are comforted (consoled and encouraged), it is for your comfort (consolation and encouragement) which works (in you) when you patiently endure the same evils (misfortunes and calamities) that we also suffer and undergo. And our hope for you (our joyful and confident expectation of good for you) is ever unwavering (assured and unshaken) for we know that just as you share and are partners in (our) sufferings and calamities, you also share and are partners in (our) comfort (consolation and encouragement).

For we do not want to be uniformed, brethren, about the affliction, and oppressing distress which befell us in (the province of) Asia and how we were so utterly and unbearably weighed down and crushed that we despaired even of life (itself). Indeed, we felt within ourselves that we had received the (very) sentence of death, but that was to keep us from trusting in and depending on ourselves instead of on God Who raises the dead. (For it is He) who rescued and saved us from such a perilous death, and He will still rescue and save us; in and on Him we have set our hope (our joyful and confident expectation) that He will again deliver us (from danger and destruction and draw us to Himself) while you also cooperate by your prayers for us (helping and laboring together with us). Thus (lips of) many persons (turned toward God will eventually) give thanks on our behalf for the grace (the blessing of deliverance) granted us at the request of the many who have prayed (2 Corinthians 1:3–11, AMP) (Wright p 38).

God is involved in our lives and reaches out to sustain us. Loss can bring people together in a way we never experienced before. Our pain creates a deeper sense of empathy and concern for the pain of others. Our losses are going to change our values. We are called to comfort one another and weep with those who weep (Wright p 39).

1st Thessalonians 4:18, "therefore encourage one another. Romans 12:15 rejoice with those we rejoice, mourn with those who mourn" (KJV).

Below, I have shared with you Seven Stages of Grief by Social work Tech. Please review:

1. Shock and Denial. Most people react to learning about a loss with numbed disbelief. You may deny the reality of the loss at some level to avoid pain. Shock provides emotional protection from being overwhelmed all at once, and this may last for weeks.
2. Pain and Guilt. As shock wears off, it is replaced with the suffering of excruciating pain. Although it feels unbearable, it is important that you experienced the pain fully and not hide it. Avoid or escape from it with alcohol or drugs. You may have guilty feelings or remorse over things you did or didn't do. Life feels chaotic and scary during this phase.
3. Anger and bargaining frustration lead to anger. This is a time to release bottled up emotions. You lash out and lay unwarranted blame for your loss on someone else, and you try to control extreme overreaction as permanent damage to your relationship(s).

4. Depression, Reflection, Loneliness. A long period of sadness may overtake you. You might realize the true magnitude of your loss, and it will sadden you. You may isolate yourself on purpose, reflect on things you did with your lost, and focus on memories of the past. You may also sense feelings of emptiness or despair.
5. The Upward Turn. As you start to adjust life with your loss, your life becomes a little calmer and more organized. Your physical symptoms lessen, and your "depression" begins to life slightly.
6. Reconstruction and Working Through. You become more functional, and your mind starts working again. You will find yourself seeking realistic solutions to problems posed.
7. Acceptance and Hope. In the last stage, you learn to accept and deal with the reality of your loss and situation. Acceptance does not necessarily mean happiness. With the pain and turmoil you experienced, you can never return to the carefree, untroubled YOU that existed before this tragedy, but you will find a way forward.

CHAPTER 11

The Cross of Shame, Fear, and Control

Take my yoke upon you, and learn of me, for I am gentle and lowly in heart, and you shall find rest for your souls. For my yoke is easy, and my burden is light.

—Matthew 11:29–30

Shame is a sense of being uniquely and hopelessly flawed. It leaves a person feeling different and less valuable than other human beings.

Shame is self-oriented. "There is something wrong with me."

Guilt is knowing that we have done something wrong. It tells us that we made a mistake.

Guilt is action-oriented. "I did something wrong."

Genesis 3:9 says, "BUT THE Lord God called to the man, 'Where are you?'"

Isn't it interesting that God was calling for Adam as if there were more people around other than Adam and Eve? But here's the irony of the question that God posed to Adam. God is still calling Adam. You and I asking us all "where are we?" You see, God and Adam were used to being in fellowship with one another. Fellowship is a friendly association, especially with people who share one's interests. Fellowship means companionship, sociability, camaraderie, friendship, and mutual support. God was use to speaking with both Adam and Eve in the cool of the Day in the midst of the garden. However, now God is inquiring Adam and Eve of their whereabouts, and they decided to hide themselves. They hid themselves because after eating the fruit of the Tree of the Knowledge of Good and Evil, their eyes were opened, and now they knew for the first time that they were naked.

Naked means a part of the body without clothes. Nude, bare, having nothing on, stripped, unclothed, and undressed. Feelings and or behavior undisguised; blatant. Plain, unadorned, unvarnished, and unqualified.

Hid means to conceal from sight; to prevent from being seen or discovered. To obstruct the view of or to cover up from the knowledge or exposure; to keep secret.

Hide means a part of the body without clothes. Nude, bare, having nothing on, stripped, unclothed, and undressed. Feelings and or behavior undisguised; blatant. Plain, unadorned, unvarnished, and unqualified.

RESTORING THE FOUNDATION

There are four different problem areas that we must visit before we are to move on and be healed from shame, fear, control, and we identify how they work. These four areas are sins of our fathers, resulting curses, idols, and ungodly beliefs.

> Thou shall not bow down thyself to them, nor serve them: for I the Lord thy God am a jealous God, visiting the iniquity of the fathers upon the children unto the third and fourth generation of them that hate me. (Exodus 20:5)

The sins of the father and resulting curses which is the Second Commandment states that God will visit the iniquities of our fathers upon us to the third and fourth generation. Some of us are going through and have been dealing with a spirit that has visited upon us or our kids as a result of our parents' or grandparents' sins. Some therapists, when they see their clients, do a genogram which is basically a family tree, but this genogram looks at a variety of things such as trends that we have in our families. Such treads could help us identify why we do what we do such as divorce, incest, abuse, alcoholism, and other trends that can be determined from having a genogram done.

If you study the genogram really closely, you can see trends or maybe understand the reason why divorce may run in your family. Granddad got divorced, and then your dad was divorced, and now you're divorced, so then you can see that their maybe a generational curse operating in your family. That's not to say that the divorces were not warranted, or they should have never been together in the first place. The genogram is showing the trend of what has occurred. Another such case would be your father was an alcoholic and you're not, but you see that your son is, and you may have seen signs of his son even at a young age starting to engage in drinking. While that may be a trend in the world of counseling, social work, and psychology, it very well maybe a generational curse operating in your family bloodline, and you have to be careful to Rebuke and Denounce the curse and take authority over it in Jesus's name!

These iniquities press or squeeze us to continue or enter into these sins of our fathers which are the sins of our ancestors.

The next thing I would like to discuss is about Idols. An idol is anything that we put our trust in other than God. That can be a person, place, or thing. For example, it's only when I come to this place (wherever that might be) do I find peace. No, our peace is in God. Our peace has nothing to do with a special geographical position or place in this world, especially when you use words such as "this is the only time I can find peace." So we have to be careful of the place we go, things, and people. I once went to a person's house, and they had bought a statue of an African figure. Well, at the time, I was taking a class on foreign religions and art culture. This figure was just like the one in my book.

I even went home and came back to make sure it was the same figure before I said anything. This figure was a figure of an African goddess. I won't say the name of the goodness but it was a "sex goddess," and it just so happen that my friend and her husband was dealing with some infidelity in their marriage. Well, coincidence, right? Maybe I don't really know. But I do know that spirits are real.

My friend got rid of the statue, to say the least. That's why the Scripture teaches us about Exodus 20:3, "Thou shall have no other Gods before me." This is the First Commandment of the Ten Commandments. Isn't it funny (okay not funny)? The irony of this Country was that it was built on the foundation of the Ten Commandments. It's true that when you read America's Constitution, you will see the Ten Commandments being played out through its entirety. But the question is, do we adhere to them? Galatians 3:13 says that "Jesus became a curse for us. Because cursed is he that hangs on a tree." So then shame, fear, and Control are very much based on the sins of our ancestors even going back to Adam and Eve.

Romans 12:2, "And be not conformed to this world: but be ye transformed by the renewing of your mind, that you may prove what is that good, and acceptable, and perfect, will of God." With ungodly beliefs, we need to have God's truth instead of the lies we believe about ourselves. Remember earlier I told you that when I was younger, my sister told me I was adopted. Well, I found out that that's not uncommon when you have older siblings to say certain things and tell lies to their younger brothers and sisters.

But here lies the problem: I believed her because I looked up to my older sister, and why would she lie? She is three years older than me, so she should certainly know whether or not I was adopted. I grew up in a very close-knitted family. However, even though she did not think that the effects of her lie would cause me any harm, the Devil used it to attack me most of my adolescent life, and then couple that with my dad's death. I was at loss without having a sense of identity or knowing who I was. Do you see the picture now? Even though it was a lie that my sister told me, I always felt less than even after I was told by my mother that I was not adopted. The Devil was attempting to steal my identity, and thus, it caused me to live in shame for years. I did not ask my mother about me being adopted until I was grown because I was ashamed of who I was and fearful of who I was not.

We all grew up in families. Some of us grow in other people's families. Nonetheless, it was a family. Sometimes, you received soul seer hurts from family members like I did because they're hurting themselves and launch out and attack you because they don't understand their own selves. Family members hurt people. And hurt people hurt good people. In a true sense, you hurt the ones you love because they are the closest people for you to hurt. You don't hurt strangers because they're not close enough to you to even care whether you hurt them or not. We, in general, hurt the closest people to us. A lot of our ungodly beliefs come from our family members. Luke 4:18 says that Jesus came to heal the broken hearted, those scars, tears, wounds, and bruises. Isaiah 53:4 says, "Surely he hath borne our griefs, and carried our sorrows: yet we did esteem him stricken, smitten of God, and afflicted."

"But He was wounded for our transgressions; he was bruised for our iniquities: the chastisement of our peace was upon him; and with his strips we are healed" (v 5). That's why God wants us to offer ourselves and not animals (Old Testament) as living sacrifices. Our daily living, aside from our own desires, should be to follow him, putting all our energy and resources at his disposal and trusting him to guide us. We do this out of gratitude that our sins have been forgiving.

God has good and pleasing plans for His children (Jeremiah 29:11–13). He wants us to be new people with renewed minds living to honor and obey him since He wants only what is best for you and since we should joyfully volunteer as living sacrifices for His service. Christians are called to "be not conformed to this world" with its behavior and customs that are usually selfish and often corrupting. Many Christians wisely decide that much worldly behavior is off limits for them. Our refusal to conform to this world's values, however, must go even deeper than the level of behavior and customs. It must be firmly founded in our minds: "Be ye transformed by the renewing of your mind." It is possible to avoid most worldly customs and still be proud, covetous, selfish, stubborn, and arrogant. Only when the Holy Spirit renews, reeducates, and redirects our minds are we truly transformed.

> For they that are after the flesh do mind the things of the flesh; but they that are after the Spirit the things of the Spirit. For to be carnally minded is death; but to be spiritual minded is life and peace. Because the carnal mind is enmity against God: for it is not subject to the law of God, neither indeed can be. So they that are in the flesh cannot please God. (Romans 8:5–8)

One of the things that I realized before I was able to "deny" myself was that the enemy always wants to steal your identity. I know I touched on this before, but my goal for bringing this up again is that the Devil still does not have any new tricks. He is still playing the same old games. He is still after our identity in God.

God created us to have unique characteristics and purpose. However, he designed us also to have a commonality of contentment with our lives through His will. We discover our true identity the more closely we are drawn to Him.

Your race may be European or African American. Your ethnicity, white or black. Your nationality, American, but your identity is in Jesus Christ. The nation that forgets God is turned into hell. Righteousness exalted a nation; sin is a reproach to all people.

To be Afrocentric means I am because of my ancestors. To be Eurocentric means I am because of my Country. And to be Christocentric means I am because He is. We must let go of our Afrocentric and our Eurocentric arrogance and embrace a Christocentric intelligence and realize that "I am because He is."

Mankind has lost our identity in God, and we no longer share the image of God. That image that God made in Genesis 1:27 that states, "let us make man in our image and in our likeness." We were made in the image and likeness of God, and in a great sense, we do not look like our daddies' babies. We are like Adam because of our inability to deny ourselves. We do not resemble the image that God intended for us to have and know. Because of sin in our lives, we have to contend with the many strongholds in our lives and personalities and our emotions and our mind. A lot of us have been afflicted by those strongholds and don't know it. That's why it's important to identify what our issues are so that we can deal with them. I want you to understand that there is a spirit operating among us, and that spirit is the spirit if shame, fear, and control.

In the case with Adam, shame caused Adam to hide himself because he knew he did something wrong. But the fear of what God was going to say or do about the wrong that Adam did is what caused Him to sow fig leaves together and then hide himself because now his eyes were open to the naked truth. But it was the spirit of Control that made him think that he could cover (literally) hid sins from the face and presence of God. But think about it. Isn't that what we do even now? We do something wrong. We know if anyone finds out about it, it will bring us shame, and fear of being caught causes us to manipulate and hide or control our circumstances so that we do not get caught. As I said before, people don't stop sinning because they get caught. You stop sinning because the fire in your life gets hot. Meaning you realize that every time you do something, you no longer can get away with it. Your old tactics are not working. That's called sanctification, which is usual test in trials that come into our lives and burn righteousness (right living) inside us because we realize that God is trying to tell us something and that He is working a work in our lives that take us from being in control. But until we get to that point, we try to basically control everything in our lives.

> (Matthew 11:28) Tells us to come unto me, all ye that labor and are heavy laden, and I will give you rest. Take my yoke upon you, and learn of me; for I am meek and lowly in heart: and ye shall find rest unto your souls, for my yoke is easy, and my burden is light.

We must eliminate the sin patterns in our life, but how do we do that? We must come unto Him with all of our insufficiency and all of our inadequacies and give them to the Lord. We must always remember to deal with the truth. If you are an adulterer, bring your adulterer self to the Lord. If you are a Hoe monger, bring your Whorish self to the Lord. We must restore the foundation. We must apply a renewed mind versus the ungodly beliefs mindset that you have been operating from. We must apply the hearts hurt to a new lifestyle because of the curses of our fathers and because of us being born in the iniquity of our families.

The seeds of abandonment, rejection, and abuse are seeds waiting to be triggered in an event in your life. The devil and his demons are waiting for an event to happen in your life so that they can take the sins of our fathers and the current hurts and use those seeds to trap us in **shame, fear, and control.** Now here's the thing: the younger you are, the more hurt and more damage you can do mainly because we're not thinking yet to responding, so any event that occur trigger the seeds to start to grow. In my case, it was my sister telling me that I was adopted. Couple that with puberty and the changes my body was going through, along with the death of my father when I was thirteen, it left me with low self-esteem and low self-worth. The seeds of shame had begun to operate in my life, so I thought thoughts of: "I will always be broken. I will always be stupid. I will always be less than. I will always be dumb."

We have all had shaming events to happen in our lives. Not everyone of us had a shame-based trauma however. But things like rape, incest, abuse, rejection, or abandonment of the person who has done these things to us can cause us to be victimized, and its incredible triggers for the bases of shame. The questions that come out of these events are, what's the matter with me?

"What's the matter with me" is the essence of a shame-based mentality that we begin to adapt. The seeds that came from the sins of the father's and resulting curses come down to us, and a hurt happens, and the seeds get triggered in our mind. We begin to believe the ungodly beliefs of the enemy (about me), and the demons are hopping up and down and saying we got another one (Kystra). The devil doesn't want us to be saved, and if we are saved, he doesn't want us to fulfill our destiny in God. We become so self-focused trying to control our shame that we become pre-occupied trying to get free from whatever binds us, and we miss our appointment with God and the

Destiny that He has for our lives. As I stated to you before, I knew God was trying to get my undivided attention for years, but I knew that meant that I could not do what I wanted to, so I controlled my shame, my guilt, and my fear by not letting go and not letting God.

You can see this in the story of Samson in the book of Judges (13–17). Samson was anointed by God to be a Judge of a nation of people, but Samson lacked purpose in his life (not the purpose of God, his own purpose), so he spent most of his time chasing after women and perverted his anointing because he really thought that his strength was in his hair and not God. Some of us really think that our strength is in our jobs or 401 *K*s and 403 *B*s and our ROLFs or the stock or car or house we have. We really believe it's from how many big wigs we know and how many degrees or boards we sit on. When we really get down to it, one tragedy in your life, one loss income, one day of change like being fired from your job, it can change who most of us are. What I have found out is that my job or the car I have or the money I possess is not who I am. My strength lies in God. It was not until I lost all that I had before I really saw, who I was, and I found out who He was because I saw the real lover of my soul.

Shame is being uniquely and hopelessly flawed. Guilt is knowing that we have done something wrong. Even though guilt is present, it is predicated only after a shaming event. So we begin to ask questions like, "Why am I like this? There must be something wrong with me."

1. Why is my father (stepfather) abusing me and sexually molesting me? A little girl might ask. What's the matter with me? Why is this happening to me? We all know that our parents and family are supposed to be our protectors, our uncles, aunts, and cousins. What's the matter with me? I must be uniquely and hopelessly flawed for this to be happening in my life.
2. Uniquely means that I'm the only one like this in the whole world. That's the lie that gets stirred. That's why people who get abused in these ways don't tell other people because

they feel that nobody is going to believe me. It's my fault. Shame by its very nature will not allow me to share this with you because you wouldn't understand because I am uniquely and hopelessly flawed. I'm so bad I can't let you know about it, and flawed means that no one can fix me, not even God because he allowed or let this happen to me. Not even God can help me. Lies, lies, lies. This is who I am. Guilt will come and go as we do good things and as we do bad things, but shame will stay because I can't get rid of who I am (Kystra).

3. Shame-based person—uniquely and fatally flawed. What's their primer motivation?

- To be their own safe place. They don't trust God or other people.
- Goal is to keep shame from being exposed to keep from experiencing the pain of abandonment and rejection.
- Abandonment is the foundation on which shame sits. Abandonment triggers the shame.
- Pain that goes with the abandonment, the isolation, and the rejection is something we don't want to experience, so we push it down, we hide it, or we compartmentalize it so that we don't have to deal with the pain of it. We work hard to keep the pain of the shame from being exposed.
- Shame tells you how awful you are, and it stirs fear because people will find out what happened, and they are going to judge and reject you or blame you, so you begin to control the fact that no one must know to keep them from finding out.
- There is a synergy that these three spirits together make them worse than if they were just working individually on their own. We often get mad when people are able to see our stuff, but that only makes us hide even more.

- Shame traps us like no other stronghold does because Shame prevents us from being who we really are! We're trapped, we're different, and we're flawed. I'm too big. I'm too small. I'm too tall. I'm too short. I'm too black. Or I'm too white. I have short hair. I got long hair. I'm too skinny. Or I'm too fat. Control is the Sherriff to make sure that everything is under control and peaceful. The Sherriff cuts down anyone that threatens the Shame or Controller who argues you down that they got it all together or the passive person who hides and won't take any risk to expose their shame by saying "I'm just screwed up and nobody can help me" to themselves. Or the perfectionist who says, "If I do everything just right, give my tithes, come to Bible class, and be at Church every Sunday, then nobody will discover how awful I really am."
- Genesis 3:6 says that Adam and Eve's eyes were open, and they realize that they were naked. They lost their Crown of Glory. They were shamed that they could see their nakedness. So what did they do? They sowed fig leaves together as a covering for themselves. They took control and said we will keep God from seeing our shame.
- Adam and Eve hid and controlled their circumstances. Why? Because they were ashamed. They learned to distinguish good and evil, and they were ashamed. They had been naked before they ate the fruit, and there was no shame there.
- Adam told God, "I didn't answer you because I was 'afraid.'" There's the fear. "Why, Adam?" "Because I was naked. There's the shame." God said, "Who told you that you were naked? Did you eat from the tree that I told you not to eat from (disobedience)?" And Adam and Eve took control, and they hide themselves.
- What have the human race done for years where we have to hide ourselves? But the question is, why?

> Could the answer be "I don't want you to see who I really am!"? I don't want you to see that I am uniquely and utterly flawed, and I don't want you to see it because I can't do anything about the way that I am. I can't be fixed.

Over time, we have trained our words not to believe what we say and not to believe with what the truth is (God's truth). So if you keep telling yourself that you are stupid and that you are flawed and that you need fixing, then eventually, that's what you will begin to believe. Proverbs 23:7 tells us that as a man thinks in his heart, so is he. But God loves us just the way we are—tattered and torn and hurt and bleeding and frustrated and fractured in our emotions because Jesus already died for all of our sins and trespasses. Jesus already died for our healing, and with His help, we can move forward out of shame, fear, and control.

Chapter 12

Follow Me

*Jesus said to his disciple, "whoever wants to be
my disciple must deny themselves
and take up their cross and follow me.*

—Matthew 16:24

To **follow** means to proceed or come after or to enlarge in a calling or way of life. To follow also means to pursue and to be or act in accordance with. Follow means to accept and to come to a place after a certain period of time to obey.

According to Matthew 16:24, "If any man is to come after me he must take up his cross and follow me." Following Jesus is a day-by-day journey, which includes relying on Him to lead the way. At times, following Jesus can be a difficult thing to do. There are so many distractions in our world that are trying to compete for our attention and loyalty. Many of which are easier to do.

Even though to follow Christ sounds simple, it takes a stronger man or woman to follow Christ than it does to not follow Him. Following Christ means that you are living for something bigger than yourself. It means that we have to watch what we say and what we do.

Following Christ has to do with letting go. Let go of anything that will hinder your progress of getting to know God. Galatians 5:7 states, "You did run well but who did hinder you?" Who is stopping or hindering you from having fellowship with God in a way you have never perceived God to be before? Most of the time, we know what's wrong with us and why we cannot fully and truly surrender ourselves to Him.

It is impossible to be a good leader without being an even better follower. Leadership has to do with promoting a set of values or system that can be used to motivate or cultivate people or a product. But how can we ever be a great leader when we refused to follow, and if we do follow, we want to follow based on our terms. Peter, Andrew, James, and John were all fishermen. Fishing was their job. Following Jesus begins with seeing yourself as a helpless sinner. This is very important, and there are many people who have difficulty with this point. In our human nature, we want to believe that there is something good about us. We are told to "believe in ourselves." But the Bible says each one of us has sinned (Romans 3:23). The Bible teaches us to deny ourselves (Matthew 16:24).

I have a question. How many times would a person have to steal a car to be considered a thief? One time, right? Likewise, it only takes one sin to be a sinner. A sin is any wrong action or any wrong thought (Isaiah 59:7; Matthew 15:19). The great news is, Jesus came to save sinners. He came to find the Lost. He came to heal the sick (Luke 5:31–32) (Bible.org).

Following Jesus means that you have faith. Following Jesus means that you trust him to provide everything you need. Philippians 4:19 says:

> My God will supply all you needs according to His riches in Glory in Christ Jesus." Everyone needs his or her physical needs taken care of; Jesus proved to Peter that he provides everything we need. One day Jesus was standing by the Sea of Galilee. The people crowded around Him and listen to the word of God. Jesus saw two boats at the edge of the water. They had been left there by the fishermen, who were washing their nets. He got into the boat that belonged to Simon (Peter).

Jesus asked him to go out a little way from shore.
Then He sat down in the boat and taught the
people.

When Jesus had finished speaking, He turned to Simon (Peter) and said, "Launch out into the deep, and let down your net so you can catch fish" (Luke 5:1–4). Remember, Peter had toiled all night trying to catch fish and did not catch any fish. Now Jesus is telling the fishermen to launch out into the deep to catch fish, dropping his net on the right side of the boat. Peter had just washed his nets. If he let them down into the sea again, the nets would be full of salt water, and Peter would have to wash them all over again. Peter told Jesus that he had been up all night trying to catch fish, but Jesus told him to put his net down in deep water. Peter trusted then obeyed.

Often times, God will tell us to do something that may be out of our way or seem too hard at the time. However, we must always be like Peter—obeying and trusting Him. There is a blessing in obedience, and even if you don't see it immediately, it is always better to obey God no matter what He tells you to do. God always rewards those who trust Him (Bible.org).

When they had done so by casting their nets into
the deep, they caught so much fish that their nets
began to break. So, they motioned to their partners in the other boat to come and help them.
They came and filled both boats so full that they
began to sink. (Luke 5:5–7)

When Peter saw the miracle that Jesus did, Peter fell at Jesus's feet and said, "Get away from me, Lord. I am a sinful man" (Luke 5:8). Peter realized that Jesus was God, and Peter worshipped Him right there in that smelly boat filled with fish. This was a huge step for Peter in becoming a disciple of Jesus. When Peter realized that Jesus was God, everything changed!

Jesus told Peter not to be afraid, and from that time forward, instead of catching fish, Peter would now catch men. This meant that

Peter would join Jesus in telling people about the Kingdom of God. This would be a huge change for Peter. He had been a fisherman all his life. It's what he knew how to do and how he made money for his family. Can you imagine Jesus telling you to drop everything you normally do to go do something totally different like "following Him"?

Following Jesus means that we must listen, obey, and do things His way. Jesus came to invite lost people into God's Kingdom. If we are going to follow Jesus, then we must listen, obey, and be careful to do things His way. Peter and his friends had to leave fishing behind as their career. Though they were good at fishing, Jesus had a much bigger and better plan for them. When you are a true disciple of Jesus, He may tell you to do things differently than what you did before (Bible.org). Jesus is everything that we need. If you are to follow Him, you must listen to what he is saying to you now.

Everyone needs forgiveness from sin. Jesus even provided the way of eternal life to those who put their faith and trust in Him. When we lack faith, it is often because we don't trust that God will provide exactly what we need. Jesus proves to us that He is our faithful Provider. Faith is based on knowledge and experience. We know that we can trust God because of how we've seen Him work in our lives.

In order to follow Jesus, we may realize *that* some of us cannot reach our potential because we are no longer teachable or willing to follow. We have what I call the "I'm-grown" syndrome. That's where nobody can tell you what to do. You won't take advice and you won't seek wise counsel, but when you do, you don't apply the things needed for you to change.

What does it really mean to follow Christ? First of all, there must be a desire to follow him. John 15 tells us that "if you abide in me as my words abide in, then you may ask what you will, and it will be given unto you." But he goes on to say that "without me, you can do nothing!" We really can't be fulfilled with God's plan for our lives without Him. Proverbs 19:21 says, "There are many devices (plans) in a man's heart, but the counsel (purpose) of the Lord it shall stand." God made us to be in fellowship and to bring pleasure to Him by being a living sacrifice, holy, and acceptable, which our reasonable service is. Matthew 4:24-25 says:

> News about him spread all over Syria, and the people brought to him all who were ill with various diseases, those suffering severe pain, the demon-possessed, those having seizures, and the paralyzed; and he healed them. Large crowds from Galilee, then Decapolis, Jerusalem, Judea and the region across the Jordan followed Him. (KJV)

Jesus had a crowd with some desiring to follow Him. Some desired to follow Jesus because of all the miracles that He was performing. It was their chance to be healed and set free from what had kept them bound for years. Their desire, however, was based upon the excitement and what Jesus could do for them. Maybe Jesus would heal them or bless them or turn water into wine today or "multiply my earnings today or bless my fish and my bread so that I will have even more loaves of bread to bring home."

They wanted to follow Jesus, but it was for the wrong reasons. In Matthew 16:24, Jesus elaborates on what He means by following Him when He said, "if any man would come after me, he must deny himself, and take up his cross and follow me." How many of you know that you can find God while you're sitting on a bar stool? You can find God after an argument with your spouse. You can find God in the middle of your abuse, but the question is, will you "follow Him"? That doesn't mean that you will not cry sometimes or that you're not going to hurt, but every day with Jesus is sweeter than the day before!

It is in these words that you find the heart of the Christian Gospel, deny yourself, take up your cross, and follow Him. It is here that the Great Commission of Matthew 28 is seen where Jesus tells his church to go and make disciples—that is, "Make people follow you because you are representing and modeling me." You've been trying to show folks that you are blessed and highly favored. You've been trying to dictate to your friends and family that God is with you because you got a new car. But the fact remains that going to church no more makes you a Christian than going to McDonald's makes you a hamburger. What makes you a Christian is your desire to FOLLOW Jesus.

Following Jesus means that I'm going to have to put things of God ahead of my own fleshly desires. It means I'm going to have to do some introspection on me and deny myself of the things that turn me away from God. Following God means that for some of us, God has brought you into your NEW season in your life, and you are going to have to let go of the old places, old things, and old relationships in order to embrace the NEW. To do that, you got to Praise God in advance for what He is doing and about to do in your life. Some of us in order to follow Christ, we must do what the Apostle Paul did. "Forgetting these things which are behind and reaching forth to those things which are ahead, we got to PRESS, it's going to be a fight but we got to press toward the mark for the prices of the HIGH calling of God in Christ Jesus" (Philippians 3:14). The Apostle Paul said that:

> That I have been following Christ but I had to work much harder, I've been in prison frequently, I've been wiped more severely, I've been exposed to death again and again. Five times I received from the Jews the forty lashes minus one. Three times I was beaten with rods, once I was stoned, three times I was shipwrecked.
>
> I spent the night and day floating in the open sea. I have been constantly on the move, I have been in danger from rivers, in dangers from bandits, in danger from my own countrymen, in danger from the gentiles; in danger in the city, and in danger in the suburbs, in danger at the sea, and in danger from false brothers and haters that would lie on me. I have labored and toiled and have often gone without sleep; I have known

> hunger and thirst and have often gone without food; I have been cold and naked. Besides everything else; I face daily the pressure of my concern for all the churches. (2 Corinthians 11:23–28)

So being a Christian has not been easy because you must adopt standards that are not the world's standards. But through it all, I have learned to trust in Jesus. I have learned to trust in God.

Some followed Jesus out of curiosity. They heard the stories about Jesus from others, and they wanted to see for themselves what was going on. They did not follow Jesus because they wanted to commit themselves to Him, but rather, they followed Him to satisfy their own curiosity. Some followed Jesus because they hated Him. Most of the people who hated Jesus were the church folks—the Pharisees and Sadducees—the ones that were supposed to know God hated Him to His face. They wanted to end His life and shut Him up. They didn't care what He was saying or what He was doing. To them, His message was trouble, and they could not accept it as truth. They listened and took notes only to use them against Him at a later time because their desire was to destroy Him. But there were some who followed Jesus and were following Him for the right reason. They witnessed what He said and what He was able to do, and they were drawn to Him. They wanted to get to know Him better. They wanted to be friends with Him. They wanted Him to be a part of their lives, and they wanted to be a part of His. They followed Him because they loved Him. Even after they heard what it would cost them to follow Him, they still wanted to follow. Jesus told them what it would cost them, and then He called the crowd to Him, along with his disciples, and said, "Whosoever wants to be My disciple must *deny* themselves and take up their cross and follow Me."

Jesus begins to tell His disciples and all those that were around that the "Son of Man must suffer many things and be rejected by the elders and the chief priest and the scribes and be killed, and after three days, he shall rise again."

Jesus knew the path that He had to walk, and He did so in faithful obedience. And He did not hide this path from His followers. He was very open and honest with them about His death and resurrection. Even so, it must have come as a surprise to His followers as He was explaining this plan to them.

After the crowds followed Jesus to the other side of the sea, the Bible tells us that as the people caught up with Him, they asked Jesus to explain to the crowd that He is the bread of Life in St. John 6:41–71, and the Jews then murmured at him because he said that he was the bread which came down from heaven. And they said, "Is not this Jesus, the son of Joseph, whose father and mother we know? How is it then that he saith, I came down from heaven?"

It amazes me that these men who were scholars in the law, the canon Word of God, could not discern who Jesus was. They really think He is just Joseph and Mary's baby. Verse 43 says that Jesus therefore answered and said unto them, "Murmur not among yourselves. No man can come to me, except the Father who sent me draws him: and I will raise him up at the last day." (There it is right there, you all. God must draw you to stop doing what you want to do and DENY yourself.)

You know God has been tugging at your heart. You know God has saved you time and time again from your foolish self. Verse 45 says:

> It is written in the prophets, and they shall be all taught of God. Every man therefore that hath heard, and hath learned of the Father, cometh to me. Not that any man hath seen the Father, save he which is if God, he hath seen the Father. Verily, verily, I say unto you, he that believeth on me hath everlasting life.

"I am the bread of Life. Your fathers did eat manna in the wilderness, and are dead. This is the bread which comes down from heave, that a man may eat thereof, and not die" (v 49).

"I am the living bread which came down from heaven, if any man eats this bread, he shall live forever: and the bread that I will give is my flesh, which I give for the life of the world" (v 51). "The Jews therefore strove among themselves, saying, how can this man give us his flesh to eat? Then Jesus said unto them, Verily, verily, I say unto you, except you eat of the flesh of the Son of Man, and drink his blood, you have no life in you" (v 52).

I know the religious rulers got to think that Jesus is tripping. "What? You mean, we got to eat of your body and drink your blood? This is cannibalism."

Jesus goes on to say in verse 54, "Whosoever eats my flesh and drinks my blood, hath eternal life; and I will raise him up at the last day. For my flesh is meat indeed, and my blood is drink indeed."

"He that eats my flesh and drinks my blood, dwells in me, and I in him. As the living Father hath sent me, and I live by the father, so whosoever eats me, even he shall live by me" (v 56).

"This is that bread which came down from heaven: not as your fathers did eat manna, and are dead: he that eats of this bread shall live forever. These things said he in the synagogue as He taught in Capernaum" (v 58).

> Many of his disciples when they heard this, said, "this is a hard saying: who can hear it?" When Jesus knew in himself that his disciples murmured at it, He said unto them, "doth this offend you? What and if ye shall see the Son of Man ascend up where he was before? It is the spirit that quicken; the flesh profited nothing: the words that I speak unto you are spirit and they are life. But there are some of you that believe not" for Jesus knew from the beginning who they were that believed not, and who should betray him. And He said, "Therefore said I unto you, that no man come unto me, except it were given unto him of my Father. From that time many of his disciples went back, and walked no more with him."
>
> Then said Jesus to the twelve, "WILL you also go away?" Then Simon Peter answered him, "Lord, to whom shall we go? Thou hast the words

of eternal life. And we believe and are sure that thou art that Christ, the Son of the Living God."

Jesus answered them, "Have not I chosen you twelve, and one of you is a devil?" He spoke of Judas Iscariot the son of Simon: for he it was that should betray him, being one of the twelve. (St John 6:60–71)

There comes a time in everyone's life, I believe, that they have to make a very important personal and individual decision. It's a choice that every human is offered. It is a choice to follow Christ or not to follow Him. He paid a price that you could not afford to pay. He died on a cross for your sins. He was pierced for our transgressions and bruised for our sins. Forget all the other blessings that come from following Christ and remember that the punishment that brings us peace was upon Him and when He went to the Cross, we were healed. With that in mind, I want to know: do you want to FOLLOW HIM?

CHAPTER 13

Put God First

Jesus looked at him and loved him. "One thing you lack;
he said." Go, sell everything you have and give to the poor,
and you will have treasure in heaven. Then come follow me.

—Mark 10:21

In order to truly follow after God, we must learn to put Him first. We do that by seeking after Him. Webster defines to "seek" as to attempt to find something. It means to search for, try to find, look for, be on the lookout for, be after, hunt, and be in quest of. It also means to attempt or desire to obtain or achieve (something). It means to ask something from someone, request, solicit, call for entreat, beg for, petition for, appeal for, apply for, and to put in for. But all of this has to be done by seeking God first. You have to remember whenever purpose is not known, abuse is inevitable. You will continue to abuse yourself and your purpose until you learn how to "deny" yourself. Take up your cross and follow Christ. So let's see what the Word of God has to say about seeking God.

Matthew 6:33 says, "Seek ye first the kingdom of God and His righteousness and all the other things, shall be added unto you." When you seek the Lord, you are seeking for His presence. "Presence" is a common translation of the Hebrew word "face" (Bible Dictionary).

Literally, we are to seek His FACE. But this is the Hebraic way of having access to God. To be before His face is to be in His presence.

First we must realize that God is omnipresent, and therefore, He is always near everything and everyone. He holds everything in being. The Scriptures tell us that through Him, all things were made. Without him, nothing was made that was made (John 1:3). Colossians 1:16 says, "For in him, all things were created: things in heaven and on earth, visible and invisible, whether thrones or powers or rulers or authorities; all things have been created through him and for him" (King James Version).

His power is every present in sustaining and governing all things. He is always present with His children in the sense of his covenant commitment to always stand by us and work for us and turn everything for our good (Romans 8:28).

"Behold, I am with you always, even to the end of the age" (Matthew 28:20).

There are times when we may feel as though God's presence is not with us. For this reason, the Bible repeatedly calls us to "seek the Lord; to seek His presence continually. God's manifest, conscious, and trusted presence is not our constant experience. There are seasons when we become neglectful of God and give Him no thought and don't put our trust in Him, and when we do that, we will find Him to be unmanifested in our lives. That is unperceived as great and beautiful and valuable by the eyes of our heart.

His face, the brightness of his personal character, is hidden behind the curtain of our carnal desires. Romans 8:1–8 tells us that:

> Therefore, there is now no condemnation for those who are in Christ Jesus because through Christ Jesus the law of the Spirit who gives us life has set us free from the law of sin and death. For what the law was powerless to do because it was weakened by the flesh, God did by sending his own Son in the likeness of sinful flesh to be a sin offering. And so, he condemned sin in the flesh in order that the righteous requirement of the law

> might be fully met in us, who do not live according to the flesh but according to the Spirit. Those who live according to the flesh have their minds set on what the flesh desires; but those who live in accordance with the Spirit have their minds set on what the Spirit desires. The mind governed by the flesh is death, but the mind governed by the Spirit is life and peace. The mind governed by the flesh is hostile to God; it does not submit to God's law, nor can it do so. Those who are in the realm of the flesh cannot please God. (Holy Bible, NIV, 2011, Bible Gate Way)

Carnal is translated from the Greek word (sarikikos), which literally means fleshly. Every time we sin, we are acting carnal. The key thing to understand is that while Christians can be, for a time, carnal, a true Christian will not remain carnal for a lifetime. So you see now, and I hope you understand that until you "deny" yourself and get out of your flesh, you can't even please God.

Seeking God is always continual, and this condition of the flesh is always ready to overtake us. That is why we are told to "seek His presence continually." God calls us to enjoy continual consciousness of his supreme greatness, beauty, and worth. We do this by presenting our bodies as living sacrifice holy, acceptable unto God which is our reasonable service, and being not conformed to this world but being transformed by the renewing of our minds, that we may prove what is the acceptable, and perfect will of God is (Romans 12:1–2).

I hope you're starting to see this theme here, and that is, you cannot please God in the flesh. After Adam and Eve fell into sin in Genesis 3, you see them having to leave the Garden, but they are now aware of good and evil and right and wrong, and they are wearing skin that God gave them to cover up their nakedness. This skin could be considered the first sacrifice of blood for mankind, and later, you will see that Jesus Himself came to be the sacrifice with the shedding of His blood to reconcile the world back to God. However, these skins also represented this skin suit that we wear daily called the "flesh." The flesh is a sin suit and a reminder that we need God daily in everything that we do because if we walk in the flesh, we cannot please God.

When God said:

> "Let us make mankind in our image and in our likeness, so that they may rule over the fish in the sea and the birds in the sky, over the livestock and all the wild animals, and over all the creatures that move along the ground." So God created mankind in his own image, in the image of God he created them; male and female he created them. (Genesis 1:26–27) (Bible Gateway, Holy Bible, NIV, 2011)

After the sin and fall of man, God had to cover over and cover up the Glory of His Image and gave man a sin suit called flesh because man lost the image of God when he fell into sin. A restoration of this image is taking place in believers through the work of the Holy Spirit as we submit ourselves to God by 'denying" ourselves. The full restoration will be completed in the resurrection.

You and I are the principle creature on earth. Although we occupy this planet with animals, fowls, of the air, creatures in the seas, and moving creatures on the ground, we are the principal creature on this earth. We were made in the image and likeness of God. God formed man out of the dust of the ground, and that's why when we die, we go back to the ground.

But God formed man with a rational soul and made him the ruler of the earth. We still are the image of God even though that image has been marred by sin. But being the image of God means to be like God in actions, appearance, thought, and character. Man was able to enjoy the spiritual perfection of God and possesses it by deliberate choice. Hebrew 2:6–8 tell us:

> What is man, that thou art mindful of him? Or the son of man, that thou visitest him? Thou has

> made him a little lower than the angels; thou crownest him with glory and honor, and didst set him over the works of thy hands: Thou hast put all things subject under his feet. (Gruits, p 33)

We were made to rule, but when we sin, we lost all authority to do it in God's way. Now you have to make a conscience choice to choose God.

Both the Old and New Testament says to seek the Lord is setting your mind and heart on God. It is the conscious fixing or focusing of our minds' attention and our hearts' affection of God.

Chronicles 22:19 says, "Now set your mind and heart to seek the Lord your God."

Colossians 3:1–2 says, "If then you have been raised with Christ, seek the things that are above, where Christ is, seated at the right hand of God. Set you mind and affections on things above, not on things of this earth. We must seek ye the Lord while He may be found call ye upon Him while He is near."

The apostle Paul prays for the church in 2 Thessalonians 3:4 by saying, "May the Lord direct your hearts to the love of God and to the steadfastness of Christ." It is a conscious effort on our part to seek the Lord. But the effort to seek God is a gift from God because before you ever thought to seek God, God had already pursued you and placed in you the desire to seek after Him. We do not make this mental and emotional effort to seek God because He is lost. We don't seek God like we lost a valuable coin or a shoe. God is not lost. We are. We seek God because we need God to meet us where we are at. For some of you, that may be in your hurt, in a broken relationship, in financial ruin, and it may have meant that someone hurt you or messed over you and dropped you like hot rocks. But the urge to seek God comes from the inside of our heart to know Him, to want Him, to understand Him, and know His will for your life.

There are endless obstacles that we are to avoid in order to see God clearly and so that we can be in the light of His presence. We must make a conscious effort to get through the natural means to God himself to constantly set our minds toward God in all our experiences to direct our minds and hearts toward him through means of His revelation. This is what seeking God means. The Scriptures teach us "that the natural man receives not from the Spirit of God neither can he know them because they are spiritual discerned" (I Corinthians 2:14). When you are in your flesh, you can't understand the things of God. You can know the Bible backward and frontward, but if you're not walking in the Spirit, you do not understand that everything moves by the Spirit of God.

We must flee spiritual dullest. We must move from stumbling blocks. We must stop allowing other people to make us stumble and fail at God's Word. We know what makes us vitally sensitive to God's appearances in the world and in the Word. We know what dulls us and blinds us and makes us not even want to seek Him. We must move away from the things that stop us from denying ourselves. We have to cry out to the Lord in prayer for His guidance and His deliverance. Isaiah 55:6 says, "Seek the Lord while He may be found; call upon him while he is near."

"For you will seek God and plead with the Almighty for mercy" (Job 8:5).

Seeking God involves calling and pleading. O Lord, open the eyes of my heart. Lord, I want to see you, to see you high and lifted up shining in the light of your Glory. Open up your mercies of love as we say holy, holy, holy, holy, holy, holy, I want to see you. Don't you want to see the Lord? I know I do!

We have to remember that seeking God is not about stuff and things. It's about seeking His presence, His Will, and His Kingdom to come on earth as it is in heaven. Webster says that a kingdom is a country whose ruler is a king or queen. In the spiritual world of which God is King, we are to seek "first the kingdom of God and His righteousness," which means to turn to him first for help or deliverance. We must fill our thoughts and heart with the desires to seek the king, to take his character for your pattern, and to serve and obey him in everything. People, objects, goals, and other desires all compete for priority in your life. Any of these things can quickly bump God out of first place in your life if you don't actively choose to give him first place in every area of your life.

Seeking the kingdom of God is not a place. Seeking the kingdom of God is a lifestyle as a method of living which Jesus Christ prescribed for His body the Church. It's a prescription. For a dying world, it's a requirement. It's a method of discipline and self-denial that produces the fruits of the Holy Spirit in our lives. Then Jesus said unto His disciples, "If any man will come after me, let him deny himself, and take up his cross and follow me. For whosoever, will save his life shall lose it, and whosoever will lose his life for my sake shall find it" (Matthew 16:24–25).

There is a purpose for this lifestyle. The purpose of the kingdom lifestyle is to conform us into the IMAGE of God's son and to make us partakers of His holiness. Romans 8:28–29 tells us:

> And we know all things work together for the good to them that love God and to them that are called according to His purpose. For whom He did foreknow, he also did predestinate *to be conformed to the image of His Son*, that He might be the firstborn among many brethren.

Denying yourself and following God is about you getting the image of God back into your life through surrendering your body, soul, heart, and mind. Leviticus20:7 tell us to "sanctify yourselves therefore, and be ye Holy: for I the Lord your God is Holy."

The Kingdom of God's lifestyle produces those fruits that are a part of our mind, love, joy, and peace. These special qualities affect man's relationship with his neighbor: longsuffering, kindness, and doing good produces three Christian conducts: honesty, gentleness, and temperance. For the Bible says in Galatians 5:22–23, "But the fruit of the spirit is love, joy, peace, longsuffering, gentleness, goodness, faith, meekness, temperance: against such there is no law."

If we are to seek God, He requires us to live Holy lives in peace with all men as much as possible. Hebrews 12:14 says, "Follow peace with all men, holiness without no man shall see the Lord."

God wants us to discipline ourselves to seek after Him. Discipline is what is required in the local church and is the training we receive from those in authority over us. It is designed to train character through instruction, control, correction, and strengthening. II Timothy 3:16–17 says that all scriptures are given by the inspiration of God and is profitable for doctrine, for reproof, for correction, and for instruction in righteousness that the man of God many be perfect and thoroughly furnished unto all good works. Discipline teaches us obedience through submitting our will to the will of God. Hebrews 13:17 says, "To obey them that have the rule of over you and submit, unto them for they watch for your soul, as they must give account, that they may do it with joy, and not with grief, for that is unprofitable for you." We must learn obedience because God demands it of His children. He does not only require us to obey in keeping His commandments, but we are to practice obedience in every area of our lives.

Regardless of what you have been through or what you have done, God has made up His mind about you, and you are worth saving. And his problem is, now that you're worth saving, He wants to show people your worth in Him. The people that have hurt you are the ones that God wants you to protect even though they have instigated some of your pain. Joseph's assignment was to protect his haters. His haters were his own brothers. They hated him because God gave him a dream that one day, they would bow before him, but Joseph's problem, if any, is that you can't share your dreams with everyone because they can't handle what God has shared with you.

However, if Joseph had not shared his dream, he would have not gotten sold into slavery, and if that didn't happen, he would had never worked in Potiphar house. And if that never happen, he would have never got tempted by Potiphar's wife. And if that didn't happen, he would have never ended up in jail, and if that didn't happen, he would have never interpreted the king's dream, and if that didn't happen, he would have never been left in jail only to interpret the king's dream again only to be exalted and pardoned from his jail sentence to be the second ruler in kingdom. And if that did not happen, when the famine hit the land, he would have never been in position to help his father and brothers. And if he never was in position to help them, then they would have never bowed down before him. And if they never bowed before him, then he would have never had to dream the dream that they would. So everything has a reason and a place in your life. Your abuse may have never caused you to seek help from God, and if you never did that, you would have never been able to deny yourself. And if you did not deny yourself, you would have never fulfilled God's plan for your life and your family.

So then if you have no haters, then you're really not that gifted because, you see, only gifted folks and blessed folks can cause someone to hate you for no good reason at all. When God formed Adam from the dust of the earth and breathed into Adam the breath of life, Adam became a living Soul. God is breathing on you right now. He is calling your life to come back into your body. Breath in the Greek is translated "Ruach." It is the life force of God. You thought you lost it because of what you have been through, but when you begin to deny yourself, you will see God in a whole new light.

"To everything there is a season and a time for every purpose under heaven" (Ecclesiastes 3:1). It's your season to rise up Adam and to rise up Eve. So when God came to speak to Adam in the cool of the day, He wasn't coming to speak to him in his emotions. He was speaking to Adam in His mind (spirit). He was communing with Adam's spirit just like He communes with us now. After the fall, God stopped coming to Adam in the cool of the day. We now have to come to God, but once again, it's to communicate with Him in our Spirit. It was during the fall that Satan, being the god of this world, was able to deal with us in our sensory realm. That's why the first thing the devil wants is to get control of your mind. Because we are born into sin and shaped in iniquity, Satan has a jumpstart on dealing with you in the area of your senses because he uses your sense to keep you from operating in the spirit realm. Have you ever wondered why you don't have to teach a baby to sin? That happens automatically, but you do have to teach a baby (child) to do what's right because we are born with a sin nature, but must we get the nature of God? You can tell a person who has been changed by God because their nature has changed. The things they use to do, they don't do anymore.

In my spirit, I'm God conscience. In my body, I'm self-conscience. And in my mind, I sense conscience. So then my relationship with God is not physical. It's spiritual. See? It was in the cool of the day that God came to visit Adam (spirit) mind, but when Eve was created, she was created from Adam's body. That's why women have the parts needed for a man to fit into like a puzzle to become one because we only need that for the body, self. God is never recognized. He is always revealed before the fall of man. God could come visit us. Now we can boldly come before the throne of grace that we may obtain mercy in our time of need.

Whatever you may experience in your childhood, Satan has always used it negatively to hopefully wreck you as an adult, so when you get to the place and time when you meet Jesus or give your life to Him, Satan wanted you to be so messed up emotionally, mentally, physically, and spiritually that you missed your chance to deny yourself because of all your pain and your loss, and you lose out totally to the will of God in your life. That's why for some of you, Satan wants to control your mind by having you chose to use some mind-altering substance life alcohol or marijuana or drugs because he knows you have to have a right mind to choose God. Satan wants to alter your mind. But what you don't realize is that God don't wait for you to come out the fire. God will get in the fire with you and deliver you while you are still in the fire of your life decisions. It's not that God can't bring you out of your circumstance, but God wants you to have joy in your circumstance knowing that He is able to bring you out of all of your problems. You have got to learn when God delivers you. You got to replace the hurt, the drugs, and the abuse with reading and studying the Word of God so that you won't have a slight healing as we discussed before because if you move to fast, you will have thoughts born out of you through negative things that have happened to you. You have to change your thinking to change the direction your life is going in, and you do that by submitting yourself to God and by seeking first the kingdom of God and His righteousness, and all the other things will be added unto you.

Finally, my brothers and sisters, whatsoever is true, whatsoever is honest, whatsoever things are just, whatsoever things are pure, whatsoever things are lovely, and whatsoever things are of good report, if there be any virtue and if there be any praise, think on these things (Philippians 4:8, KJV). In order to think on these things, you got to put God first and follow Him.

Chapter 14

Entering into the Will of God

Following Jesus is easy when life runs smoothly; our true commitment to God is revealed during trials. Jesus assured us that trials will come to His followers. I have told you these things that you might have peace. In this life, you shall have tribulation: but be of good cheer I have overcome the world. (John 16:33) Discipleship demands sacrifice, and Jesus never hid the lost.

The plan is to get to Canaan. It is the place that the Hebrews journeyed to which was the Land of Promise. This land of Canaan belonged to Abraham's descendants, and they begin this long and painful and even disappointing journey to set off to go to this land.

Genesis 12:1 says, "Now the Lord said to Abram, get thee out of thy country, and from thy kindred, and from thy father's house, unto a land that I will shew thee:"

I don't know about you, but what God said to Abram sounds like an eviction notice, and He wants him to vacate the premises. If you are to enter into the *will* of God for your life, the first thing you must learn to do is *obey*. First Samuel 15 teaches us a clear lesson that obedience is better than sacrifices.

1. Disobedience is an act of rebellion.
2. Disobedience is sinful.

3. Disobedience is a form of idolatry.
4. Disobedience disrespects God's word.
5. Disobedience is based on looking good to other people rather than to God.

Obedience is better than sacrifice because God attaches a lot of benefits to your obedience. Job 36:11 says, "If you obey and serve Him, they will spend their days in prosperity and their years in pleasure."

There seems as though there is always a season of separation from folks, friends, and your family before you can get the Blessing from God. In other words, there is a process that you may be going through right now. As I said it before, for some of you, it may be sickness, a bad relationship, dealing with abuse, rejection, or abandonment, but you got to remember it is a process to get you to the promise, so God can initiate your purpose. There always seems to be a disgrace before the grace and a putting on and taking off of something to get to the next level in your life.

Abraham was raised in a Pagan culture that believed in many gods. God knew that for Abraham to stay in his country with his family would be detrimental to his spiritual growth. In fact, his family and friends would help to hinder his growth in God. You have to watch out for folks that are friends with the world after the have degreed that they are now saved.

In Luke 9:62, Jesus said to the man who wanted to delay following Him because of his family that "no one, having put his hand to the plow and looking back, is fit for the kingdom of God." In the same way, God was essentially saying to Abraham, "You have to make a clean break." You have to leave now if you are going to move forward spiritually. If you are going to enter into the will of God, you got to let go of some things and people who you know have normally held you back or you have held onto just because. Philippians 3:13 says, "brethren I count not myself to have been apprehended but this one thing I know, forgetting those thing s which are behind and reaching forth to those things which are ahead, I press toward the mark for the prize of the high calling in Jesus Christ" (KJV). It's hard letting go of things and people and stuff that make you comfortable. It's hard to break out of your comfort zone to step out on nothing. That's why Abram was called the friend of God because He staggered not at the promises of God, and it was imputed unto him as righteousness (right living) before God.

You will never reach your destiny no matter of your ability, giftedness, or purpose if you do not make the conscience decision to let go of the world and to follow Christ. Average is all you will ever be, and you will never reach your spiritual maturity. 1st Peter 2:2 says, "As newborn babies, long for the pure milk of the Word, that you may grow thereby." Verse 3 says, "If so, you have tasted that the Lord is gracious" (KJV).

The spiritual strong holds that people have had on your life for years will be broken when you let them go. You have got to get your soul back. You have allowed sin to run (ruin) you. You have allowed too many people in your solace realm, and now you have got to get their fingerprints off your soul. How do you do that? You leave them alone and separate yourself. Even in AA, Alcoholic Anonymous, and NA, Narcotics Anonymous, they tell you leave old things and people that will cause you to relapse alone. Even in rehab, they will get you clean from the substance or addition by keeping it away from you while you go through chemical and emotional withdraws for more than thirty days. But within that thirty days, you have to replace that emptiness of not using or drinking with positive reformation be saying and doing any and everything that will prevent you from relapsing. Sometimes, it takes two and three times in rehab before you finally make up your mind that "this time, I'm going to do it. I'm going to change my nature because healing occurs from the inside out, not the outside in."

Genesis 12:2 states that God promised to bless Abraham, and God said:

1. I will make thee a great nation.
2. I will bless thee.
3. I will make thy name great.
4. Thou shall be a blessing.

5. I will bless them that bless you.
6. I will curse them that curse you.
7. And in you will all the families of the earth be blessed.

God promised to bless Abram and make him great, but there was one condition. Abram had to do what God wanted him to do. This meant leaving his home and his friends and traveling to a new land where God promised to build a great nation from Abram's family. Abram obeyed, walking away from his home for God's promise of even greater things in the future. God may be trying to lead you to a place of greater service and usefulness for him. Don't let the comfort and security of your present position make you miss God's plan for your life.

The timing of Abraham's call by God was significant. It occurred shortly after the destruction of Babylon and the dispersion of the nations. Humanity had done its best, and God brought plans for the future to nothing. Yet God's plan for Abraham was still "I will make you a great nation; I will bless you and make your name great; and you shall be a blessing" (Genesis 12:2).

The Lord's commands are rarely accompanied by reasons, but they are always accompanied by promises. There are times when God will speak to you and tell you to do this or that, and at the time when He tells you, it does not make sense, but then overtime, we see the revealed manifestation of if later. When the Lord told Abram to leave his family and country, it didn't make sense at that moment. But he would later understand the plan and purpose of God. The Lord was essentially asking Abram to trade one thing, and He would give him something else in its place. But God's trade in deals is not the same as what we would expect from other people. God was saying, "Abram if you leave your old land and your kin folk, I will give you nations that will speak of your name for generations to come."

What is it that you know you must leave? Take a moment and really think about what it is that if you left it, it would give you great freedom. Now I'm not talking about you leaving your husband or your wife and then saying that brought you joy. I'm talking about a stronghold that you have been dealing with in your life, and you may have been able to kick it or leave it for a while, and you end up going right back to it. It may be an old relationship that you know is not going anywhere, or maybe you want to stop eating everything you see and diets are not working. Or maybe it's been an abusive situation that has caused you a lot of hurt, pain, and shame, but you just can't seem to let it go. Or maybe you just can't seem to forgive the person that wronged you or hurt you. In your head, you forgive them, but they do one more dumb thing or just seeing them or hearing about them or God knows being in their presence, is only going to show you even greater why you have not forgiven them because they said they changed. It appeared that they've changed, but when the right situation comes up, you see the same old them. I just want to say that same old them might be that same old you.

God tells us to turn our backs on sin and to turn away from people who could drag us down spiritually. If we do, He will bless us. Unfortunately, this is not what Abram did. Abram sort-of obeyed God but not completely. God told him to leave his country, separate himself from his relatives, and go to a land that God will show him. Abraham did leave his country, but he did not separate himself from his family nor did he go straight where God told him to go.

We read that Abram took his Father, Terah, and his nephew Lot. The name **Terah** means "**delay,**" and it was a delay for Abraham. Webster defines the word delay as to make someone or something late or slow. To detain, hold up, make late, slow up, slow down, postpone bog down, or suspend. What has God told you to do which you have been in the spirit of delay? Oh, yes. God, I'm going to do it. I'm going to get to it. You just may be delaying your blessing. Remember all of those blessing that we discussed previously that Abram was going to get if he moves where God told him to go? Well, he still was going to get them, but by taking his father with him, it resulted in a "delay," and the delay resulted in at least a five-year-delay in a place called **Haran** which means "**parched.**" Webster describes the word parched as dried out with heat, extremely thirsty, scorched, dehydrated, and burnt out. Some of our stuff, family, friends, and significant others had burned us out. Until Abram obeyed God in what he previously had been told, we read of no further command from God.

What I want to bring out is that Abraham himself was not disobedient, but when you try to take people with you into your blessing, it doesn't always work out the way you think it should.

Two things are important to note. First Sarai was childless—a catastrophe for a woman in the ancient world. Secondly, that Lot was Abram's orphaned nephew whom he seems to have adopted. He accompanied Abram, and it looks as though he would have been his heir if Sarai had not had a child. Genesis 11:31–32 shows them leaving UR on their way to go to Canaan, the Promised Land, but the entire family moved after God's command from UR an important center of culture in southern Iraq to Haran in eastern Syria. There, Terah died. Abram must have left his father, Terah, on Haran sixty years before he died (Genesis 12:4, King James Version) (New Bible Commentary). Leaving his homeland and family was a much greater decision in a traditional society than in today's mobile individualistic culture. Abram risked everything he held most dear to obey God's call. Christ similarly challenges people to venture everything to **follow Him**.

Verse 2–3 sums up the theology of Genesis and provide the key to its interpretation (see chapters 12–50). Later we see that Sarai found herself in Pharaoh's harem (15). From the way the story is told (19), it is clear that Abram's behavior is not commended. Nevertheless, the Lord intervened and rescued him by sending plagues on Pharaoh so that Abram, like his descendants, escaped from Egypt greatly enriched (Exodus 12:35–36). This mini-exodus from Egypt foreshadows its greater successors (Exodus 12–4; Luke 9:31). It shows God fulfilling his promise to protect Abram (12:3) despite his unbelief. God graciously overrules even the mistakes of those he has called to their long-term benefit (45:5–8; Romans 8:28) (New Bible Commentary).

Verse 4 says, "Suggest that God called Abram in Haran not Ur. The Land of Canaan comprised the territory currently (1993) held by Israel, Lebanon, and part of southern Syria. Abram's obedience was rewarded by an enhancement of the promise, a land that I will show you (1) becomes this land, (the introduction on the theology of chapters 12–50). God's gracious promise prompted Abram to repeated acts of thankful worship. He built an altar (7, 9, New Bible Commentary).

So you see, we need to do God's will in God's way and in God's time. Psalm 121, says, "I will look until the hills from where my help comes from, my help come from the Lord who made the heaven and the earth."

If you want to really know how to enter into God's presence, the Scriptures teach us to "enter into His gates with thanksgiving in our hearts, and to enter into His courts with Praise, we are to say this is the day that the Lord has made we will rejoice for he has made us glad" (Psalm 100:4).

You can have trouble on all sides just like the story of Jehoshaphat in the Bible in 2 Chronicles 20:1–15. The enemies of Jehoshaphat is closing in on him for the kill, and Jehoshaphat comes to that point that many of us so easily reach which is frustration. It's the point of frustration, desperation, and utter helpless. He cannot even think of a plan of action. His position and that of his people is beyond anything that he can cope with. His confession stark yet one that many of us have learned in verse 12, "neither know we what to do: but our eyes are on you Lord." As I stated, have you ever been in a situation where you really just didn't know what to do? You were tapped out, your strength was gone, and you were at you whiz end. Well that's where Jehoshaphat was at, when he got word that a couple of his supposed-to-be almost friends decided they were going to attack him and his nation.

Jehoshaphat was in the "valley of decision." You may be there too. None of the choices he was to make were going to be good. Matter of fact, he did not know what to do. Is this your position today? Is your soul crying out, "I just don't know what to do"? Have you ever not known what to pray for what to ask for? Have you felt that your life was unbearable, and to tell you the truth, you really did not know what to pray for. If so, you sound as if you are in the valley of decision just like Jehoshaphat.

The dictionary defines a valley as being an elongated depression or low-lying area between two higher ridge points. One Hebrew definition of a valley refers to a "deep place" that exists between two parallel mountain ridges. The Bible often uses topographical imagery of "valleys" to transmit an overview of a prophetic theme. For instance, the prophet Ezekiel was given a vision of a dry valley of dusty bones to portray a symbol of the house of Israel wandering in world exile, which is pictured far away from the imagery conveyed about the Promise Land being a "land flowing with milk and honey."

Valleys are also depicted as low points in the timeline of history between major epic events. People often refer to great emotional-filled times of spiritual highs as mountain-top experiences and refer to other times when they experience deep depression and anguish as a valley or low-point in life. The ironic thing about valleys is that while you are in the valley, you can see the highpoints of the mountains seen only in the distant horizon. That's right before you get your blessing. You can see your blessing, and your position of being in the valley is what has allowed you to see what God has in store for you that is coming. Before you can get to your mountain-top experience, you have your valley experience. Before you can get your blessing, you must first learn how to Praise God in the valley. You have got to understand that the same God that is over the mountain blessing experience is the same God that is the God of the valley. There is no sense of trying to wait to get out of what you're in before you Praise Him. You're going to have to praise Him right where you are.

Jehoshaphat jumped up and stood up in the temple and prayed. There was only one place for him to turn. Sometimes life is like that, and when you are facing death and eternity, God was the only one he could turn to. God is the only one who can make a difference. Jehoshaphat name means "Judge" or the "Lord Judges." Sometimes, God will allow us to be in circumstances where He has to judge us. I know that sounds kind of harsh, but the reality is, I would rather God judge me down here than for Him to judge me up there. Down here, I still got time to get it right. Up there after death, comes the judgment. You are either stuck in your righteous or stuck in your wrong. So God judging me down here is a good thing.

After Jehoshaphat's prayer, the Lord spoke through His prophet Jahaziel and said, "Listen all of Judah and the inhabitants of Jerusalem and King Jehoshaphat: thus saith the Lord to you. 'Do not fear or be dismayed because of this great multitude **for the battle is not yours, it's the Lord**.'"

There it is right there. This battle called life is not yours. It's the Lord. It is the Lord that gives to you His great pleasure. Being confident of this one thing that He that started a good work in you shall also perform it until the day of Jesus Christ (Philippians 1:6). "Thanks be unto God which always causes us to triumph in Jesus Christ" (2 Corinthians 2:14).

"You will not need to fight in this battle set yourself to "stand still and see the salvation of the Lord" (v 17).

"And appoint you some singers unto the Lord and send them out to the battle field first" (v 21).

This is what I call and known as a Pre-emitted Strike which is similar to what happen to us on 911, but the difference is, this strike is on the enemy. You have got to send up a Pre-emitted Strike of Praise on the enemy. Judea means Praise, and Judea and Jerusalem was facing an enemy bigger than them. The Bible says that Jehoshaphat sent the Praise Team out to fight against the other armies and they began to sing. "The other armies began to have a fight among themselves, God set an ambush for the enemy and they killed themselves without Jehoshaphat or anyone from Judea or Jerusalem ever throwing a fist punch, knife blow against them or anything" (v 22).

So in your valley experience, it could be that the one thing that God wants from you is for you to Praise Him, Love Him, Seek Him, Adore Him, Trust Him, and put Him first by denying yourself.

The Bible goes on to say the next day that they went into the enemy's camp and took all of their gold, silver, and precious things. Even off their dead bodies, they had so much stuff that they had to come back the next day. It's time to go into the enemies' camp and take back all that he stole from us. He may have stolen your joy. It's time to get it back. He may have stolen your peace, your mind, your man, and it's time to get your stuff back. How are we going to do it? We are going to give God some praise.

The Bible says in verse 26 and on the fourth day that they assembled themselves in the valley of Be-ra-chah: which was translated in Hebrew that means as the Blessing.

The reason why you're fighting is because the enemy knows that you're in a valley in your life, and he thinks you're going down this time and not getting back up, but what he didn't know was that we are standing in the valley of Be-ra-chah: which means in the Hebrew "we are standing in the Blessing and in a Bless place and on bless ground." I know it was bad two weeks ago, but now I'm getting myself together, and I'm dusting myself off because I am sick and tired of being sick in tired, and God said, "I'm standing on Bless Ground. The enemy being trying to get you to move from your blessed ground. He been trying to get you to shift your values on motherhood, but that's bless ground. He been trying to get you to go back to the old way you dealt with people and relationship which was abuse of your purpose, but you got to tell the devil, "I'm about to set a Pre-emitted Strike on you." Somebody please help me praise the Lord. You ought to turn on your Gospel music and starting cleaning house, make sure you open up the door and put the Devil out because he doesn't live here anymore.

As I said to you before, my life was spiraling out of control. I had just lost my grandmother in January, in July one of my sons passed away, in August my mother fell into a comma for now known reason, in September I lost my job, in March my wife passed away, and a few months after that, another son passed away. I was losing all that I had, and now I was homeless. What was I to do? It seemed as though I was in the "spirit of delay." But you got to know in your spirit when God's hands are on your life and when you have been anointed for an assignment in your life, it will bring Glory to God. Even though you may be suffering right now and you feel like you're delayed from your blessing, remember, delay is not denial. You have just entered into God's will by following Him. And all God wants is for you to have the proper response and praise.

CHAPTER 15

Psalm 31:15, My Times are In His Hands...

My times are in His hands; deliver me from the hands of my enemies, and those who pursue me.

—Psalm 31:15

Timing is everything. The difference between a good joke and a bad one is timing. Time is essential when dealing with people. Timing is important in cooking. How long you leave something in the oven and it cooks well has to do with timing. If you catch a problem early, you will be able to treat it more effectively. Your timing is important in taking your medication. If you take your medication as directed, it will be helpful. If you take extra doses, it can be deadly. Timing is important in finance. The time when you invest in a particular stock and when you sell the particular stock will make the difference between whether you make money or lose it. Timing is important in your spiritual life as well. It is critical to live your life with an acute awareness of God's timing for your life.

In Ecclesiastes 3:1–15, the writer of the book tells us that life is really a matter of timing. This should be evident to us. You and I probably have a dozen of clocks and few calendars in our homes. Many of us carry or wear a watch, and we have indicators of timeline on our phones, computer screens, and laptops. Time and timing are everything because timing releases the power and presence of God in our lives like never before. We know what time it is, but we have not discerned the season for our purpose or for us to come out of whatever binds us from God. In Verse 15 in Ecclesiastes, we see time as being an opportunity. The writer's thesis is this: "There is an appointed time for everything, and there is a time for every event under the heaven. Now, to me, this is good news because that means that there is an expiration date on your test and trials, trouble, and pain. Trouble will not last always. The keyword in this section of Scripture is "time," and it is used thirty times in Ecclesiastes 3:1–8. There are three insights that I would like to leave with you today.

The first is that the writer, probably Solomon, is not going to be making judgments on the topics that follow in 3:2–8, and he is merely recording the events that occurred "under heaven." Second, Solomon builds his argument upon the word "appointed." The events of our lives do not randomly happen by chance. God has a purpose behind them. Third, Solomon uses and unusual Hebrew word translated "event." This word conveys the idea of "delight." By using the word "delight" instead of one of the standard's nouns, Solomon implies that there is a good sense of success based on appropriate timing even if the activity, by its nature, is not delightful. In other words, no matter what is going on in my life or how bad or how good it gets, I can find God in whatever time or season that I am in my life.

What I discovered as I was dealing with the pains of losing all that I had loss is that God had already prearranged times of increase and times of blessings. You will have opportunities to meet the right people, opportunities to advance in your career, and opportunities to fulfill your dreams. You may not be experiencing any good breaks right now. Maybe you're stuck in a rut. But let me encourage you with this: in your future, there are God-ordained moments. He has them planned out for you. Too many times, people miss these moments like I did for years not "denying" myself, so God could take me on another level in my life, and people try God, and if they fail for various reasons, they quit believing. Or they get distracted. Or there is so much clutter in their lives they can't hear the small still voice inside telling them that "it's your moment of Favor."

We have to be sensitive to God's timing. We may go for years with nothing big happening, and then all of a sudden, a God-ordained moment comes along. You may meet someone who changes your life. I did. You may get a loan to buy the house of your dreams, and you may be promoted on your job. In a split second, like my earlier stories of David, you go from being a shepherd boy living out in a field to being a champion of God living in a Palace. I love when David said in Psalms 31:5 that "my times are in your hands." Isn't that good to know that God got all of the times that we need to move forward, to learn, grow, mature, be blessed, and successful? All of our victories are in God. Job said it well when he said, "All the days of my appointed time, I'm going to wait until my change comes." It's amazing for me to know that my change is coming, but when it comes, you must have the "courage to change."

David and Job were saying, "God, I know you have supernatural breaks planned out for me. God, you have the right people; the right opportunities, so I don't have to be stressed out. I will stay in peace knowing that you will get me to my final destination, and that final destination is walking in the will and favor of God.

After everything that I lost, it was all a lesson to be learned from my losses. One of the most important things that I can tell you to help you get through your loss is that God looks at the response to the things that you have lost. I know that sounds hard to process, but in essence, what I am saying is, give God the proper response to whatever it is that you have lost. Praise Him in the good times as well as in the bad times. First Thessalonians 5:18 says, "In everything give thanks for this is the will of God in Christ Jesus concerning you." Everything that I lost, God restored: house, car, job, finances, and God even blessed me to get married again. But you got to remember, most of all, that "our times are in His hands."

Conclusion

I started at Destiny School of Ministry a year ago because I felt a tug in my Spirit by the Holy Spirit to go back to school to receive my doctorate. For me, at first, I did not know what my next step would be in life. However, I wanted to be in God's will regarding whatever it was that I was to do next in my life. The last four years have been very difficult—losing my grandmother in January of 2013, losing one of my sons in July of the same year, and then my mother falling into a comma for no known apparent reason. Then a month after that I lost a great-paying job all while my wife was in the hospital with heart disease, and then six months later, she passed away followed by another son passing away the same year.

It was in the same year in November 2013 that the Lord spoke something in my Spirit that burns in my heart daily, and that was Matthew 16:24: "If any man is to come after me, let him deny himself and take up his cross and follow me." That word DENY was like a neon sign that sounded like "STOP. That burned in my spirit." So I began to do research on the Scriptures and what it meant to deny yourself. Deny basically means to stop doing what you want to do. I felt at that time that was something that I could not do without the help and guidance of the Lord.

Who tells grown folks what to do? Or who is it that you may know that don't do what they want to do? We live in a society where people are always doing what they want to do. Over the next few months and years leading up to now, I would learn what it meant to deny myself.

I soon learned that I had a lot of anger and bitterness inside of me from my past hurts and pains that others had given me as well as the many self-inflicted wounds that I gave and received of myself. Fast forward, coming to Destiny every class spoke to me right where I was hurting, paining, praying, and praising. The love of God has used my classwork as therapy sessions to create in me a body of work of healing and reconciliation unto Him.

Every class I had helped me to locate myself because I had a navigation problem. And my spirit was saying deny, but like on any navigation system, when you go off track, it says "recalculating." The classes and the assignments challenged me. It would not let me stay in grief or loss or pain any longer than what God was permitting me to be. Destiny caused me to look at how I judge others and really never forgave them for the wounds that I feel they gave to me through this tumultuous undertaken of death and loss and knowing or even understanding my indemnity or who I was apart from the people that were in my life. I could not believe when I purchased the *Inner Healing Teaching Series*. I felt like "God, you got jokes. You knew I needed this." I had recently found a church that provided inner healing classes, and I was attending them regularly. However, to have the tapes and material in my hands at my disposal, how much better could it get? I felt as though God was being so specific with me and providing me with what I needed to move forward into His will for my life.

Through my experience and the writing of this book, I was challenged with letting go of some past hurts and pains, wrongdoings that were afflicted on me, and those that I held on to for dear life, so I could at least feel something. Hatred and bitterness are real, and I had a grip on them for the purpose of having something to feel and make me come alive when I thought about what the person and persons had done to hurt me, some deliberate and others not; but my bitterness and hatred was a pulse in my body that I could feel.

Forgiveness is a part of healing. The benefit of forgiveness is a gift to you from you. I realized that I was focusing on the wrong thing and wrong people. I had taken my eyes off of focusing on God. I'm writing this book to share with everyone that reads it that

Jesus truly is the way. I recognize that I have to die daily just as the Scriptures say—repent, turn around, forgive, and love my brothers and sisters in the kingdom.

I want to thank God for putting a burning in my spirit to deny myself. I want to thank Jesus Christ for giving his life for mine as a ransom for my eternal freedom. I want to thank the Holy Spirit for realizing we must put God first in everything including what we don't see that can cause harm in us the most.

I would like to conclude with a poem by Bonnie Mohr:

> Life is not a race—but indeed a journey. Be honest. Work hard. Be choosy. Say "thank you," "I love you," and "great job" to someone each day. Go to church; take time for prayer. The Lord giveth; and the Lord taketh. Let your handshake mean more than pen and paper. Love your life and what you've been given. It is no accidental—search for purpose, and do it as best as you can. Dreaming does matter. It allows you to become that which you aspire to be. Laugh often. Appreciate the little things in life and enjoy them. Some of the best things really are free. Do not worry, less wrinkles are more becoming. Forgive, it frees the soul. Take time for yourself—plan for longevity. Recognize the special people you've been blessed to know. Live for today; enjoy the moment.

Works Cited

1. In Class Study Material. Year 7 Term 4. Destiny Christian School
2. Bennett, Rita. *You Can Be Emotional Free.* Gainesville, Florida. Bridge-Logos, 1982.
3. Bennett, Rita & Dennis, and Dennis. *The Holy Spirit & You.* Alachua, Florida. Bridge-Logos, 2007.
4. Connor, Kevin J. *Interpreting the Scriptures*, 1983.
5. Guthery, Helena M. Repentance Stands Between the Church and God. National Books Inc., 1995.
6. Gruits, Patricia Beall. *Understanding God and His Covenants.* Rochester, Michigan. PeterPat Publisher Inc., 1998.
7. Greenwood, Rebecca. *Let Our Children Go.* Lake Mary, Florida. Charisma House/Charisma Media/Charisma House Book Group.
8. Kystra, Chester and Betty. *Shame, Fear, & Control. Study Lesson Series*, 2015.
9. Mohr, Bonnie. *Poet, Artist.* The Bonnie Mohr Studio.
10. Roberson, Carol, et al. *His Name... What's His Game?* Copyright 1983.
11. Savelle, Jerry. *The Favor of God.* Ventura, California, USA. Regal from Gospel Light, 1982.
12. Townsend, John Dr. & Cloud, Henry Dr. Grand Rapids, Michigan. Zondervan, 1992.
13. Unless otherwise indicated, all scriptural quotations are from the King James Version of the Bible.
14. Webster Dictionary College Press Addition, 2002.

15. Wenham, G.J. et al. *New Bible Commentary*. Nottingham, England. Inter-Varsity Press, 1994.
16. Williams, Brain K. *Sanctified Sexuality*. Sermons Excerpts, 1998.
17. Wiersbe, Warren W. *Nelson's Quick Reference Bible Commentary*. Thomas Nelson, 1991.
18. Wright, Normal H. *Recovering from Losses in Life*. Grand Rapids, Michigan. Revell a division of baker Publishing Group.
19. Scripture references marked NIV are taken from the HOLY BIBLE, APPILCATION LIFE BIBLE, and King James Version. Tyndale House Publishers, Inc. Wheaton, Illinois 1996.

About the Author

Sr. Pastor Dr. Sax Guthery Jr. has been pastoring at the Pure in Heart Church of Deliverance for over twenty-eight years. Over the years, Sax has established a number of community-based programs. The first one being CHIP, a prison-based ministry that brought the Word of God to inmates all across Michigan; Operation GROW, a program that enhances the lives of youth and increase family relationships; Unity in the Community, a program that focuses on getting youth in the neighborhoods connected to church through health screening and blood pressure monitoring and through celebrity participation. Sax developed At-Risk Program for Youth, That More Abundantly Single, Married, and Family seminars focusing on strengthening our relationship with God our spouses and the social interactions we create.

Dr. Sax and his wife, Teresa, opened up a business with the help of the Lord called Heavenly Escape & Day Spa LLC, providing services through facial, massages, makeup, and other pampering services as well as ministering to the clients that God sends. In addition, Dr. Sax Guthery is a Board Certified licensed professional counselor who provides mental health, developmental health, and psychoeducational counseling.

CPSIA information can be obtained
at www.ICGtesting.com
Printed in the USA
LVHW040931101120
671142LV00002B/93